THE
Nostradamus Code

THE
Nostradamus Code

The Lost
Manuscript
That Unlocks
the Secrets of
the Master Prophet

Ottavio Cesare Ramotti

Translated from the Italian by Tami Calliope

Destiny Books
Rochester, Vermont

Destiny Books
One Park Street
Rochester, Vermont 05767
www.gotoit.com

LIBRARY OF CONGRESS CATALOGING-IN-PUBLICATION DATA
Ramotti, Ottavio Cesare.
[Scienza temporale e papi del futuro illustrati da Nostradamus. English]
The Nostradamus code : the lost manuscript that unlocks the secrets of the Master
Prophet / Ottavio Cesare Ramotti ; translated from the Italian by Tami Calliope.
p.   cm.
Includes index.
ISBN 0-89281-666-X (hardcover : alk. paper)
1. Nostradamus, 1503–1566. Prophéties. I. Title.
BF1815.N8P74713 1998   98-16398
133.3—dc21   CIP
Printed and bound in the United States

10 9 8 7 6 5 4 3 2 1

Text design and layout by Virginia L. Scott
This book was typeset in Galliard with Bodoni and Futura as the display typefaces

Destiny Books is a division of Inner Traditions International

Distributed to the book trade in Canada by Publishers Group West (PGW),
Toronto
Distributed to the book trade in the United Kingdom by Deep Books, London
Distributed to the book trade in Australia by Gemcraft Books, Burwood
Distributed to the book trade in New Zealand by Tandem Press, Auckland
Distributed to the book trade in South Africa by Alternative Books, Ferndale

Contents

Foreword

F or centuries, the cryptic, prophetic quatrains written by Michele Nostradamus in the sixteenth century have fascinated people the world over, not merely because of our unwavering interest in all things paranormal, but because so often the events predicted by Nostradamus have come to pass. The world is filled with seers and mediums, but none continues to hold the public's interest and collective imagination as does Nostradamus, the master prophet. And as the end of one millennium approaches and the beginning of a new age dawns, the predictions of Nostradamus take on a growing significance as we strain to foresee how humankind will fare in the coming century.

It seems more than coincidence that at this point in time Octavio Cesare Ramotti, a highly respected decryption expert—formerly with the Italian state police and who in *The Keys of Nostradamus** presented the first mathematically sound system for ordering the quatrains—has now unearthed in the

---

*This title is a translation from the Italian *Le Chiavi di Nostradamus*. Published by Edizioni Mediterranee, it is currently only available in Italian.

Italian National Library in Rome a previously lost manuscript written in the hand of Nostradamus. This manuscript contains eighty illustrations by the master prophet himself further corroborating Ramotti's previous ordering of the prophetic quatrains. More importantly, using an inscription left by Nostradamus on the stone of Turin, Ramotti has discovered a deciphering code that unlocks the secret texts within the quatrains, further expanding and clarifying the full messages of the prophecies that until now have remained hidden. In his characteristic enigmatic style, what Nostradamus did was create a giant puzzle, the pieces of which he left for future generations to put together.

For the first time in the English language, *The Nostradamus Code* reveals the secret meanings of many of Nostradamus's predictions, throwing the door wide open to the new millennium. By applying the code he deciphered from the stone of Turin, Ramotti shows how the quatrains, which were originally written in French, contain embedded messages from Nostradamus in Italian. Afraid of retribution from the Church during the Inquisition, multilingual Nostradamus encoded his prophecies so that their full meaning would be understood only in a future time by those prepared to use the knowledge for good rather than evil.

To preserve the authenticity of the process, the quatrains appear in this book in three forms: first in English, then in Ramotti's Italian, and finally in their original French. The decryptions presented here are the translations of Nostradamus's exact text as decoded by Ramotti along with the corresponding illustrations done by Nostradamus himself.

Did Nostradamus accurately predict events that would happen centuries later? Will his predictions for the new age come true and lead us toward a new world order? Read on and judge for yourself.

Introduction

A Voice from the Night of Time

Michele Nostradamus opened his eyes to the light two days before Christmas—the Gregorian calendar's December 23rd was December 14th at the time—at the stroke of noon in St. Rémy, a pleasant provençal village hidden in the broad valley of the Baux. It was nearing the winter solstice in the year 1503. The crucial transitional period between the medieval and the modern eras would give him no trouble at all. During this time he would express the totality of his knowledge.

Nostradamus the humanist, philosopher, and poet keenly observed the world of politics. Finding the limitations of his own country a bit constraining, he spoke Latin, Greek, Italian, Spanish, and, of course, Provençal.

Nostradamus, a man of science, dedicated himself to the study of astrology and astronomy, to medicine (which he learned in Montpellier, France), and to surgery, practiced by necessity wherever the plague had struck.

Nostradamus, the pilgrim of God—though knowledgeable about Judaism, his ancestral religion—was a practicing Catholic. He witnessed the Restoration.

The most prestigious of Nostradamus's visitors ventured from as far as the Salon de Crau, in the Farreirux district of Provence, to honor the doctor and prophet who in the stars read the great rumblings of times to come. During a visit Pope Carl IX stopped at the Salon solely to see Nostradamus.*

The Secret Images of Nostradamus

Edited by Ottavio Cesare Ramotti and Enza Massa, these mysterious prophetic paintings concerning the fate of the popes of the modern era are brought to light in an ancient manuscript left by Michele Nostradamus to his son César, who, due to the interest of Urban VIII Barberini in the seventeenth century, sent it on to a religious order in Rome. These paintings confirm the exact ordering of the quatrains.†

Made almost illegible by the ravages of time, page 83, originally unnumbered, bears in Latin the following dedication to its readers:

> To the Honest Reader,
>
> From the prophetic mosaic of the Roman pontiffs (from Urban VIII). Those preceding him are missing here by reason of the injuries of devouring time, according to the divine will, which is uttered not by possession but in sleep and not by divine inspiration in the most eminent Abbot Joachim I, but by other ways, for our forebears have sent us a soothsayer of good and scarce possession.
>
> Cino gave this in gift to the Most Eminent Cardinal Barberini who has beseeched it with the permission of the Most Reverent Abbot.
>
> The prophecies seen by the venerable Joachim . . . from Sir Ce . . . (mus) that which . . . Abbot foresaw.
>
> **Brother Cinus Beroaldus of the**
> **Carthusian librarians at Corati, 6 September 1629**

From the time of Saint Francis of Sales, who died in 1622, thirty-one papal figures (including the aforementioned saint) succeed each other (Plate 3).

---

*Christian Kert, *Nostradamus le mage de Salon.*

†In Branch XV and XVI of my previous book: *The Keys of Nostradamus—The Twenty-first Century* by O. C. Ramotti, Edizioni Mediterranee, 1991.

Pontiff Urban VIII is not pictured, but the first prophecy states that "one shall then come" soon after Saint Francis of Sales. In fact, in 1623 Cardinal Barberini ascended to the papacy with the name Urban VIII, which makes it evident that the manuscript must have been sent to Barberini before that date, when he was still a cardinal, and also before it came into Beroaldi's hands.

Beginning in 1629, an a priori interpretation and verification begins, of which certain traces remain until the reign of Pope Alexander VIII (1689–91). The next pope will be the thirty-first. According to a well-known prophecy attributed to Saint Malachia, the thirty-second pope—Petrus Secundus—will signal the beginning of a new form of Catholicism, one that is truly spiritual. This appears to indicate an extraordinary prophetic synchronicity with the actual number of popes illustrated by Nostradamus.

Page 80 (+ 2) must be considered the last in the newly discovered eighty-page manuscript that was watermarked with a lily, afterward to which were added (at the beginning) the two pages of written interpretations of the first eight figures, causing a shift of two numbers in the pagination. Beside a depiction of three women in clothing predating the seventeenth century, the following inscription appears:

> Apocalyptic predictions by Anito Efesio, prince of the painters of his epoch, later clarified by the prophetic inspiration of the Abbot Ioachim. Tommaso Guidini of Saint John's, by approval of the most pious Carthusian Fathers, copied and restored it in the year of our Lord 1343 from the corruption of time and corrosion inflicted by the conflicts of this place.

Pages 1 and 2 bear the following heading, written in a different hand than the postscript on page 83, and certainly not written before the time of the last pope cited (Alexander VIII, 1689–91):

> Vaticinia Michaelis Nostradami De Futuri Christi Vicarii Ad Cesarem Filium.
>
> **D. I. A. Interprete**

(Prophecies of Michele Nostradamus concerning the future Vicars of Christ to his son César. Interpretation by D. I. A.—Dominus Ioachim Abatis)

Seven precise profiles of the pontiffs succeeding Saint Francis of Sales follow this heading, with names, facts, and full heraldic references, as well as an eighth one left incomplete. Evidently these are clarifications of the images on the corresponding pages, according to the old pagination.

César Nostradamus, to whom his father Michele dedicated his prophecies, was one of the leading citizens of the city of Salon, and wrote a book on the history of Provence. He lived until 1631 and was most certainly alive when Cardinal Barberini, a francophile, received the manuscript.

Catherine de Medici, widow of Henry II, showered Michele Nostradamus with gifts; she allotted him a pension and in 1564 visited him in Salon accompanied by her entire court. She inquired about the future of her sons—all of whom took the throne, if only for a brief time. Possibly by request of the Medici, she also asked him about the future of the popes. She was greatly attracted by esoteric knowledge and Nostradamus prepared for her a talisman with esoteric symbols.

The compiler of the interpretations of the first eight plates asserts directly in its title that the prophecies in question were the property of Nostradamus, passed from him to his son César. The date 1343 on page 80 (+ 2) confirms that this manuscript may not have been an illustration of the quatrains but rather their source of inspiration, particularly in those concerning the papacy.

In fact the illustrated plates interpolated by the compiler show clear signs of a different epoch and a different hand. Among these, those indubitably made or confirmed by Nostradamus may be singled out by their use of the wheel of time—a symbol that also appears on his coat of arms—as well as by the particular numerical arrangement following the characteristic undulatory progression used to order the quatrains, according to the algorithm M N (Michele Nostradamus), his seal of authenticity.

One may suppose that César, responding to a request from Maffeo Barberini for Nostradamus's prognostications concerning the future popes, may have delivered or even sold them to him. Later, bibliophiles in the Vatican made appropriate restorations to them.

Confirming the antiquity of the manuscript are declarations by Beroaldo (Brother Cinus Beroaldus) and Guidini that the document was restored because it had been damaged by the passage of time. These declarations would have been impossible had they been written ad hoc by César Nostradamus. Michele Nostradamus explicitly states that he destroyed the prophetic sources available to him, inherited no doubt from Jean (grandfather of Nostradamus's mother Renata of St. Rémy) a celebrated esotericist and cabalist converted to Catholicism, councilor to King Renè. Later, he himself knew Luca Gaurico, an Italian with whom he shared a prophetic vision of the death of Henry II in a joust.

It appears that Luca Gaurico prophesied for Pope Paul III, and that after Gaurico's death Nostradamus took his place as court astrologer. Carlo Patrian, from whom I obtained this information, does not credit the destruction of the texts, of which word may have been spread deliberately to avoid the Inquisition. At any rate, Nostradamus affirmed that his predictions did not arise from "bacchanalian fury," that is, by way of diabolic possession; therefore, this document could be consulted by even the most honest Catholic reader, the *candide lector* of Beroaldo, as long as he emerged permeated by scant—and good—fury. So now we become acquainted with one of the original sources of those prophecies that have lasted for centuries.

The Abbot Gioacchino da Fiore of Celico (Cosenza c. 1130–San Giovanni in Fiore 1202) was a Cistercian mystic who in 1191 retired to Sila where he founded the monastery of San Giovanni in Fiore (or Flora) and the religious order of the *fiorensi*, whose lost rule approved Celestine III in 1196. Developed in numerous works, memorable among them the *Concordia Veteris et Novi Testamenti*, (Agreement between the Old and New Testament), his thinking centers on a transposition to the historic level of the conception of the Trinity.

According to this vision, there would emerge three epochs: that of the Father (the time of Moses, now concluded); that of the Son (next to the last); and that of the Spirit, in which the complete spiritualization of the Church would be realized, and at which point charity, liberty, and peace would reign worldwide.

His prediction was opposed by the Church, which in the Lateran Council of 1215 condemned the doctrine. But Joachinism survived until the fourteenth century and influenced both the most progressive currents of Catholicism and those of the Reformation.

From this one may infer that the paintings of Anito Efesio were inspired in the fourteenth century by the twelfth-century visions of Gioacchino da Fiore, and then integrated by Nostradamus along with those he received personally. But who furnished these predictions to the prophets and, through them, to humanity for the future centuries? Nostradamus maintained that he was more today's clairvoyant than yesterday's prophet. *Olim dicebatur propheta qui hodie dicitur videns.* He is a prophet who speaks in the name of God, and the prophets transcribed their visions "from the times of the Father," obviously different than the linear time we perceive.

In the twentieth century, Einstein brought to light the relativity of time and its strict relationship with the planet in which it manifests. Time, however, even now is an unresolved scientific question. Linear time, which we perceive and consider unique, is the result of a multiplicity of cycles interwoven in complex ways. It is similar to saying that the year is composed of days, weeks, months, and seasons; or that a symphony expresses itself in times, rhythms, and various musical instruments, each one with its own temporal rate. Today we speak of biorhythms, of circadian cycles, to point up the rhythmic multiplicity inside a single human body and, at the level of physics and mathematics, that of dimensions and hidden variables, of virtual realities, and, therefore, of invisible parallel worlds in which temporal rhythms or "times of the Father" are diverse and multiple.*

As Nostradamus himself explains, the translation of heavenly temporal multiplicity to the apparently linear time of terrestrial history is the theme at the core of all his prophetic quatrains, suggesting some keys to their arrangement and interpretation. These keys represent the principles of a multidimensional, temporal science, as yet undiscovered, but on the brink of being born—a science Carl G. Jung put forth in his theory of synchronicity. The relationship between the multidimensionality of time (time which the clairvoyant *sees*) and historic linear time is the concept I have applied to Nostradamus's quatrains, following those keys of arrangement suggested by Nostradamus himself. Mine is an empirical application that, as I shall demonstrate in this book, has remarkable and verifiable results, as well as historic validation.

In this book, the black and white plates with evident borders are faithful drawings of the originals. Those in color were photocopied from the same manuscript.

For the numbering of the quatrains linked to the plates I adopted the following form: in place of the number of the Century in Roman numerals sub-

---

*G. Conforto, *Intuitive Science* (Crisalide e Noesis, 1994).

stitute the corresponding number in arabic numerals, leaving one space in front of the progressive number. For example: C. III, 2 becomes 3 02.

Doing the necessary calculations becomes much easier on the computer—and it is a mathematical system of additions and subtractions of the quatrains' numbers that reveals their precise chronological order, corresponding to our historical time.

The quatrains of the key text also bear a chronological enumeration and a subdivision into Branches (periods) as a result of calculations carried out for the quatrains of the twentieth century and the new millenium. For example: Branch XV, 13 (10 12)

PORTRAIT OF URBAN VIII (ENGRAVING BY OTTAVIO LEONI, 1625).

indicates quatrain number 12 in Century X, which in the temporal ordering is found in Branch XV of the twentieth century, and concerns its popes. In number 13 the prophecy concerns Pope John Paul I, Albino Luciani.

For a more detailed explanation and for a greater comprehension of the keys to the ordering of the quatrains, I refer the reader to my previous book, *The Keys of Nostradamus.*

In condemning Galileo Galilei, Pope Urban VIII sanctified the division of humanity into two opposing temporal currents—one moving in a scientific direction, the other in a fideistic direction—that would perpetuate themselves until the rising of the third millennium.

GALILEO GALILEI (ENGRAVING BY CATERINA PIOTTI-PIROLI) ILLUSTRATION FROM *GALILEO GALILEI*; ACCADEMIA NAZIONALE DEI LINCEI.

With this illustrated codex Nostradamus evidently intended to warn Urban VIII that if the popes continued to support the split, the destruction of the papacy would result. At the present time, Pope John Paul II has fully restored to favor Galileo, the founder of the modern scientific method. After the new Peter (Pietrus Secundus), there will come one united in body, soul, and spirit, as is hoped for in the last plate.

The Codex of the Seventeenth Century

IVI CCCCCC

When the forked branch is seen held up by two poles
With six half-bodies and six, the verse of the sextet revealed,
The most powerful Lord, heir of the Crapuloni,
Will hold in submission to him the whole universe.

Quando il forcuto da due pali tenuto si vede
Con sei mezzi corpi e sei, delle sestine capito il verso,
Il Signore onnipotente dei Crapuloni erede
Allora a se sottomette tutto l'universo.

Quand le fourchu sera soustenu de deux paux,
Avec six demy corps, et six sizeaux ouvres,
Le tre puissant Seigneurs, heritier des Crapaux,
Alors subiugera, sous soy tout l'univers.

This quatrain, not coincidentally separate from the text of Nostradamus's *Centuries* and *Prophecies*, most probably alludes to the manuscript in question.

Renucio Boscolo affirms that the quatrain alludes to the seventeenth century, because in Latin one thousand is expressed by an M drawn like a V (the forked branch) leaning on two I's (two poles) that appear to hold it upright. The six half-bodies (seen as circles) are the six Cs, indicating six hundred years. The acquisition date of the manuscript César Nostradamus sent to the librarian priests of Rome is September 6, 1629. In this date the M representing the millenium has two extensions on top that rest on two I's. The following 6 could refer to the day.

The sestets of Nostradamus belong to Century XI and, in large part, I have found them to form the preface to the twenty-first Century. For example, in 11 53 the years of papacy are precisely indicated for three separate popes. Boscolo also considers this quatrain, not contained in the *Centuries,* to presage the advent of the Sun King Louis XIV in 1643. This certainly could be true and is not in any grave opposition to the date of the manuscript.

Personally, I hope that a king more powerful than Louis will soon grace the universe, and not even this conflicts with the spirit of temporal multiplicity informing the prophecies.

PART I

The Popes

FOLLOWING URBAN VIII AND
ENDING WITH PIUS IX

Heraldic and Historic Confirmations

There is no need to dwell overlong on the figures of past popes shown in the first twenty-six pages of the manuscript, spanning the years 1623–1845, a period of 222 years. The twenty pontiffs represented in these twenty-six pages refer to far distant and different times than our own, while our principal curiosity is reserved for the present and future. Later, however, I will examine this part of the manuscript at some length, since it is surprising how many particulars one can find in their smallest details that confirm the prophetic vision. The images correspond so clearly to the popes in question and the historical sequence of their succession is so exact that they make us consider temporal expansion as a dimension that may become accessible to us one day.

Of these 222 years, I present Plate 3, which is relative to the first prophecy. In it is a figure of a monk handing down rules to a group of monks and nuns. It is easy to connect such images to Saint Francis of Sales, founder of the Salesian order, and to Saint Joan of Chantal. Indeed, there is a painting by Noel Hallè housed in the church of Saint-Louis-en-l'Ile in Paris that

PLATE 3: A MONK
GIVES THE RULES TO
MONKS AND NUNS.
(SEE COLOR PLATE 3.)

PICTORIAL CONFIRMATION:
SAINT FRANCIS OF
SALES GIVES TO SAINT
JOAN OF CHANTAL THE RULE
OF HER ORDER.
URBAN VIII BARBERINI WILL
FOLLOW.
THIS PAINTING MATCHES
THE PICTURE BY NOEL HALLÉ
THAT HANGS
IN THE CHURCH OF SAINT-
LOUIS-EN-L'ILE IN PARIS.
(FROM BREZZI, *THE HISTORY
OF CATHOLICISM*.)

is very similar to this one and that might make an identification possible.

Ascended to the papacy in 1623, Urban VIII Barberini promoted the missionary activities of the Salesian and Jesuit religious orders in America, Asia, and Africa. Like Cardinal Richelieu, he was an advocate for the worldwide authority of the Church.

A dove with an olive branch appears in the coat of arms of Innocent X, Pamphili (1644–55); in Prophecy number 2 a dove is present next to the figure of a pope.

HERALDIC CONFIRMATION: TWO CROSSED ARMS WITH A CROSS IN THE MIDDLE AND THREE STARS.

Clement IX, Rospigliosi (1667–69), has the head of a woman sprouting from under his vestments. It is as if she is asking protection from the fury of an armed populace, hurling itself against her. Here we are dealing with the "she-demon," the ghost of Lady Olympia, a relative of Innocent X, a pope who was much disliked by the people because of his greed. Lady Olympia is one of the most famous ghosts of the capital, and today an object of considerable tourist interest (in Rome a street is even dedicated to her). For centuries she has haunted the capitoline streets by night, dressed in black veils and laughing scornfully.

Pope number 10, Innocent XIII, Michelangelo dei Conti (1721–24), with sword and whip, receives the keys to the Kingdom from the spirit of another pope. Innocent XIII publicly flogged the Jansenist heretics, condemning the Jesuits and seven French bishops. The pope who is present in evanescent form is his predecessor Innocent III, who also was a member of the Conti family.

Pope number 15 is pictured with a soldier who is threatening him with a

PLATE 18: A MONSTROUS KING ABOVE A SEA OF FLAMES. HE WEARS THE PHRYGIAN CAP AND THE EARS OF AN ASS. WHEN THE POPULIST SANCULOTTES TOOK POWER DURING THE FRENCH REVOLUTION, PIUS VI WAS TAKEN PRISONER. (SEE COLOR PLATE 18.)

HERALDIC CONFIRMATION: THREE STARS IN ALIGNMENT.

drawn sword. The soldier's sword arm, raised to strike, is held back by the arm of an angel, emerging from the stars. Between the soldier and the pope is another sword in the form of a cross. Clement XIV, Ganganelli (1769–74), bears on his coat of arms two crossed arms—one white and one black—with a cross in the middle and three stars. This plate presages the great event that was to transform the world: the French Revolution.

In fact, in Plate 18 there appears a monstrous king above the flames, wearing the Phrygian cap typical of the Sanculotte revolutionaries. In the center of the picture, the three stars are perfectly aligned, as in the coat of arms. Pius VI, Braschi (1775–99), also had three stars on his coat of arms. In 1798 he

was taken prisoner by the revolutionaries and died in 1799 in Valence.

Pope number 18, bearing an eagle with wings unfurled on his papal tiara, is being attacked by a great unicorn while protecting a small woman. Leo XII, Hannibal della Genga (1823–29), fought ruthlessly with the liberals, who despite his efforts succeeded the conservatives in England. The unicorn is the famous heraldic symbol of Great Britain, while Leo XII's coat of arms bears a great crowned eagle. Great Britain, in agreement with American president Monroe, opposed the restoration of Spanish dominion in America. In contrast, Leo XII moved for the restoration of Spain, symbolized by the protected woman.

HERALDIC CONFIRMATION:
THE MOUNTAINS OF POPE
PIUS VII, PRISONER OF THE
REVOLUTIONARIES.

The Revolution and the Restoration

8 62

When they come to despoil the sacred temple
And the greatest and most consecrated of France are profaned,
There will rise by their hand such a vast pestilence
That the vanished king will not be able to condemn the unjust.

PLATE 22: POPE NUMBER 18 WITH THE EAGLE ON HIS HEAD, BEING ATTACKED BY THE UNICORN—LEON XII, HANNIBAL DELLA GENGA, FROM GENGA, FABRIANO, THE ANTILIBERAL BISHOP OF TIRO (1823–29).

HERALDIC CONFIRMATION: CROWNED EAGLE WITH OUTSPREAD WINGS.

Quando si verrà spogliare il sacro tempio
I più grandi di Francia e i consacrati profanare,
Per essi sorgerà così vasta pestilenza
Che il re scomparso gli ingiusti non potrà condannare.

Lors qu'on verra expiler le sainct temple,
Plus grand du Rosne leurs sacrez prophaner
Par eux naistra pestilence si ample
Roy fuit iniuste ne fera condamner.

PART II

The Popes

OF THE RESTORATION

The Roman Republic of Mazzini

First French intervention and then occupation by the Savoys nullified the dreams of the republicans.

(The sample illustration on the following page is from an ancient history book written in quatrains, concerning the first occupation of Rome (1527) antecedent to the predictions of Nostradamus. Written in three languages with commentary, it is a documentation of the seige of Clement VII in the Castel Sant'Angelo and was printed by the National Library of Paris. Nostradamus adopted the same poetic form—quatrains—in which to foretell future events. Even the typographic characters are the same.)

> The city taken, Clement Pope of Rome
> Was shut away in Adrain's castle,
> But having money on his person, he paid a great sum,
> Was released and sent back to his post.

The Arrangement of the Quatrains Concerning the Conquest of Rome

The key to the arrangement and ordering of the quatrains is based on the development of an undulatory graph that follows a sinusoid curve corresponding to the strokes of the initials in Nostradamus's monogram.* In my previous book I applied this key of order to the quatrains that concern the twentieth century and to some of those relative to the year 2000. The quatrains dealing with the nineteenth century are also arranged by the same criterion. The quatrains are designated by a number composed of three figures. The criterion of order implies that all three figures follow a course similar to the N, that is, the sinecurve of the N-wave—or rather, the Nostradamic-wave—as it appears in the pictured graphs. By observing this condition, we obtain an ordered sequence to the quatrains, one that faithfully mirrors the linear historical time we perceive.

Applying this criterion to the quatrains in question in the illustrated graphs, two popes—Pius IX and Leon XIII—clearly emerge, one after the

---

*O. C. Ramotti, *The Keys of Nostradamus*. This is demonstrated in full in all the Branches of the twentieth century.

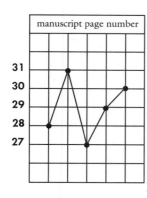

1. Quatrain 225, page **28**—Pius IX

2. Quatrain 577, page **31**—Leon XIII

3. Quatrain 350, page **27**—Occupation of the city

4. Quatrain 521, page **29**—The city taken

5. Quatrain 982, page **30**—The pope stripped of power

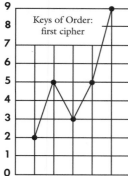

1. Quatrain **2**25, page 28—Pius IX

2. Quatrain **5**77, page 31—Leon XIII

3. Quatrain **3**50, page 27—Occupation of the city

4. Quatrain **5**21, page 29—The city taken

5. Quatrain **9**82, page 30—The pope stripped of power

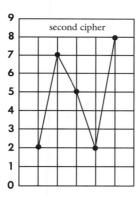

1. Quatrain 2**2**5, page 28—Pius IX

2. Quatrain 5**7**7, page 31—Leon XIII

3. Quatrain 3**5**0, page 27—Occupation of the city

4. Quatrain 5**2**1, page 29—The city taken

5. Quatrain 9**8**2, page 30—The pope stripped of power

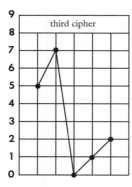

1. Quatrain 22**5**, page 28—Pius IX

2. Quatrain 57**7**, page 31—Leon XIII

3. Quatrain 35**0**, page 27—Occupation of the city

4. Quatrain 52**1**, page 29—The city taken

5. Quatrain 98**2**, page 30—The pope stripped of power

other. Analogously, the figures concerning the city of Rome are revealed in their proper chronological sequence. Finally, we are given the pope who is stripped of his secular reign. This key, which at the same time is the signature of Nostradamus, is found once again in the pagination of the manuscript that bears its own seal of confirmation.

KEY TEXT: QUATRAIN 2 25

The foreign guard will betray the fortress
And the hope, and in Umbria the semblance, of a higher unity.
The guard vanished, the fort is seized in an iron grip.
All France will fall to the outrage of death.

La guardia straniera la fortezza tradirà
Della speranza, e in Umbria parvenza, di piu alta unità.
La guardia scomparsa, nella morsa preso il forte.
Tutta la Francia sarà oltraggiata a morte.

La garde estrange trahira fortresse,
Espoir et umbre de plus hault mariage:
Garde deceue, fort prinse dans la presse,
Loire, Saone, Rosne, Gar à mort outrage.

In 1870 French troops posted to guard Rome abandoned the piazza following the fall of the Empire (consequent with the disastrous defeat in the war with Prussia). As a result, France would later submit to the outrage of a German invasion and bear the shame of not having stayed to defend the Holy See of Pius IX (1846–78).

In Umbria in the years before his ponificate, this pope reigned with great humanity from the diocese of Spoleto and his rule gave rise to great hopes of liberty in the Italian people's hearts—hopes that were later dashed. In the Vatican Council he affirmed the absolute power of the papacy by promulgating the dogma of infallibility (*The Syllabus*).

Without delay in September of the same year, the king of Italy, Vittorio Emanuele II, took advantage of the French "betrayal" to squeeze Rome and Lazio—by this time a foreign island in unified Italy—in a vise. (The wolf takes possession of the Keys of the Kingdom.)

KEY TEXT: QUATRAIN 5 77

Of the ritual of ecclesiastic honor
All degrees shall be changed in the Quirinal,
The Quirinal, rendered warlike and flaming,
Given to Vulcan by a King of France.

Del rituale d'onore ecclesiastico
Tutti i gradi cambiati al Quirinale,
Dalla fiamma che il Quirinale, bellico
Un Re di Francia renderà, e Vulcanale.

Tous les degrez d'honneur Ecclesiastique
Seront changez en dial Quirinal:
En Martial quirinal flaminique,
Puis un Roy de France le rendrà Vulcanal.

By proclaiming the Constitution of the Roman Republic, Mazzini, a hero of
the armed insurrection in the 1870s to unify Italy, abolished the secular,

PLATE 2:31: POPE NUMBER 22 DIVESTS HIMSELF OF THE TIARA OF TEMPORAL POWER AND JOINS THE FLOCK. LEON XIII (1878–1903), WITH HIS SOCIALIST ENCYCLICAL, TOOK ON THE CLOTHES OF THE PEOPLE, A HARBINGER OF THE POPULIST FACTION IN ITALY OF DON STURZO, THAT WOULD RISE AGAIN IN 1993 WITH MARTINAZZOLI AFTER THE DISSOLUTION OF THE CHRISTIAN DEMOCRACY.

governmental power of the pope, shouting, "Get the priests out of the government! Free votes!" But Emperor Napoleon III, blazing with "Vulcan's" weapons forged by the god himself—the completely new Chassepot reloading rifles of General Oudinot—initiated a chain of events that would lead to an inevitable change in the Quirinal. The seat of the popes would become the royal martial palace of the bellicose Savoyard kings.

The pope would be forced to put aside his crown and be despoiled of his lands. After Pius IX, Leon XIII (1878–1903) would "unite with the flock" with his encyclical *Rerum novarum* (all degrees shall be changed), legitimizing the unions as an expression of the popular will.

There were three flamens (the priests of Rome): the Flamen Dialis, dedicated to the cult of Jupiter the father; the Flamen Martialis, devoted to the cult of Mars, the god of war; and the Flamen Quirinalis, dedicated to the cult of Quirinus, the god of Rome.

KEY TEXT: QUATRAIN 3 50

The republic of the great city
Will not want to adapt to great rigor,
The trumpet of the exiled king inciting
The breach of the walls: the city shall repent.

La Republica della grande città
Al gran rigore non si vorrà adattare,
Del Re fuoriuscito la tromba incitare
La scalata alle mura: la città si pentirà.

La republique de la grande cité,
A grand rigueur ne voudra consentir,
Roy sortir hors trompette cité,
L'eschelle au mur, la cité repentir.

In 1849, the Roman republic did not accept defeat, although Pope-King Pius IX, exiled to Gaeta, returned with French troops. In sign of protest, Mazzini proclaimed the Republican Constitution on the Capitoline Hill and then departed for exile along with Garibaldi and others. The penetration of the city took place on June 1, 1849, at the Porta San Pancrazio gate near the Janiculum.

KEY TEXT: QUATRAIN 5 21

For the demise of the Latin Monarch
He who will reign with help and support
Will burn a brilliant fire. The Republic's
Booty divided and its bold dream disappeared.

Per il passaggio al Monarca Latino
Quello che avrà per regnare il soccorso,
Brillante fuoco si farà. Diviso il bottino
Della repubblica ardito il sogno scomparso.

Par le trepas du Monarque Latin,
Ceux qu'il aura par regne secourus:
Le feu luyra divisè le butin
La mort publique aux hardis incourus.

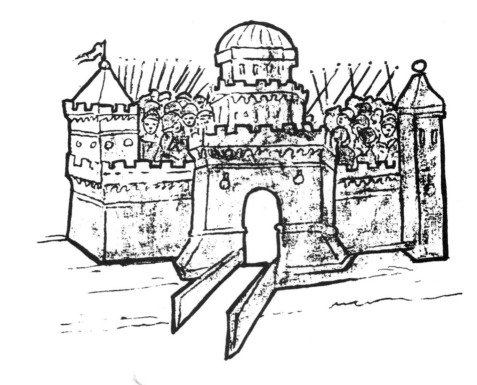

PLATE 3:27: THE CITY OCCUPIED BY SOLDIERS (1849). THE FRENCH AGAINST THE REPUBLICANS AT THE PORTA SAN PANCRAZIO GATE.

PLATE 4:29: HANDS ON THE CITY (1870). THE BREACH OF PORTA PIA AND ENTRY OF THE PIEDMONTESE INTO ROME. THE COLUMN ON THE RIGHT, PICTURED IN A PHOTOGRAPH ON PAGE 25, COMMEMORATES THE EVENT 250 YEARS BEFORE IT WAS ACTUALLY PLACED THERE. (SEE COLOR PLATE 4:29.)

Paradoxically, the king of Italy owed his reign to the help of the republicans Mazzini and Garibaldi. Mazzini dealt the first blow to the Church State of Rome by founding the Roman Republic; Garibaldi destroyed the Kingdom of Two Sicilies and handed it to Savoy on a silver platter, during the encounter of Teano. Declared the capitol of Italy in 1871, Rome was renewed "by fire." In reality it was demolished and then colonized by Piedmontese building firms and old and new nobility who changed its face and laid "hands on the city of the popes." The republican ideals of Mazzini, Armellini, Saffi, and Garibaldi were completely obliterated for almost a hundred years until the Referendum of 1947.

KEY TEXT: QUATRAIN 9 82

Through the harsh adversities of time
The great city will be long beseiged:
Sentinel and guard dead in the attack,
Taken swiftly, but not outraged.

PLATE 5:30: A NAKED KING WITHOUT SOLDIERS (1871)—THE POPES LOSE SECULAR AND TEMPORAL POWER. THE POPE IS RECOGNIZABLE BY HIS HAND RAISED IN BLESSING AND HIS TONSURE, AS WELL AS BY THE RESPECTFUL ATTITUDE OF THE CLERIC. HE IS SITTING ON A THRONE OF PETER WHICH HAS BECOME A SIMPLE WORN-DOWN STONE (PIETRA). (SEE COLOR PLATE 50:30.)

Per l'avversità del tempo forte,
La gran città a lungo assediata:
La sentinella e la guardia, per l'attacco morte,
Subito presa, ma non oltraggiata.

Par le deluge et pestilence forte,
La cité grande de long temps assiegee,
La sentinelle et garde de main morte
Subite prins, mais de nul outragee.

After a long seige of many years following the initial attempts in 1848, September 20, 1870, was the final, fatal day: the papal and Swiss guards stationed at the Porta Pia gate could do nothing against the sudden attack of the riflemen under the direction of General Lamarmora.

Nevertheless, Rome did not suffer the humiliating defeat of France; the Law of Guarantees retained possession of a portion of the city and various privileges for the pope. But Pius IX rejected the agreement with disdain and the popes incarcerated themselves voluntarily in the Vatican until the Lateran Pacts of 1929. The king remained naked.

PART III

The Popes

OF THE FIRST HALF OF
THE TWENTIETH CENTURY

I. 1903—Saint Pius X: reigned eleven years

II. 1914—Benedict XV: reigned eight years

III. 1922—Pius XI: reigned seventeen years

IV. 1939—Pius XII, Pastor Angelicus: reigned nineteen years

Key Text from the Preface to the Twentieth Century, 42

PROPHECY 11 53

Many will die before the Phoenix dies,

Until six hundred and seventy his dwelling shall endure,

Fifteen years passed, twenty-one, thirty-nine.

The first is subject to sickness.

The second to iron, danger to life.

To fire and water thirty-nine must submit.

Parecchi moriranno prima che la Fenice mora
Fino al 600-70 sta la sua dimora,
Passati quindici anni e ventuno poi viene trente nove.
Il primo è soggetto a malattia
Il secondo al ferro, pericolo di vita.
Al fuoco è all'acqua e soggetto trentanove.

Plusieurs mourront avant que Phoenix meure,
Iusques six cens septante est sa demeure,
Passé quinze ans, vingt et un, trente neuf.
Le primier est subiet à maladie.
Et le second au fer, danger de vie.
Au feu à l'eau, es subiet trente neuf.

The Phoenix represents a cycle of five hundred years, after which the mythi-

HERALDIC CONFIRMATION: THE SACRED BOOK.

cal bird rises from its ashes and a new historical cycle begins.

Six hundred and seventy probably refers to the seventy-nine pages of the manuscript for the sixteen hundreds; on page 82 (80 + 2) we have the apocalyptic conclusion with Quatrain 3 02 (Branch VI/Millenium, 23). The numbers of the Branches are according to the new ordering of the quatrains, which end up being divided into twenty-three chapters (or Branches) for the twentieth century and six more chapters for the twenty-first century, with a preface for each century.

Fifteen, twenty-one, thirty-nine: Benedict XV ascended to the papacy in 1914 (the fifteenth year from the beginning of the century), Pius XI in 1922 (after twenty-one years), and Pius XII in 1939. Above all else, the troubles of these popes were caused by World Wars I and II and the dictatorships in Russia, Italy, and Germany that tormented the first half of the twentieth century.

To Nostradamus, water represented the ebb and tide of destiny, concretized by fire (military invasions).

KEY TEXT: BRANCH VI/MILLENIUM, 5 QUATRAIN 1 54

Two turns taken by the grim reaper,
Both kingdoms and centuries are changed:
Insert the moving sign in its place,
Equal couples of right inclination.

Due giri fatti della maligna falciatrice
Di regni e secoli fatta permutazione:
Il segno mobile al suo posto inserisce
Le coppie uguali e di giusta inclinazione.

Deux revolts faits du maling falcigere,
De regne et siecles fait permutation:
Le mobil signe à son endroit si ingere,
Aux deux esgaux et d'inclination.

PLATE 35: THE WHEEL OF
DESTINY, BOTH OF NATIONS
AND OF THE PAPACY. POPE
25 ON THE LEASH OF
FASCISM. AN EAGLE
HOLDING A PAPAL TIARA
ABOVE A ROUND PLATE. THE
ANIMALS AND MEN
SYMBOLIZE THOSE NATIONS
UNDERGOING THE GREATEST
CONFLICTS OF THE CENTURY.
(SEE COLOR PLATE 35.)

PIUS XI, ACHILLE RATTI
(1922–39) OF DESIO-MILANO.

HERALDIC CONFIRMATION:
EAGLE WITH CIRCLES. POPE
RATTI USED TO SAY, "IT WILL
NOT ALWAYS GO ROUND LIKE
THIS," IMITATING THE
MOVEMENT OF A WHEEL
WITH HIS HANDS. HE BLESSED
THE PEOPLE FROM A WINDOW
OF HIS VOLUNTARY VATICAN
PRISON UNTIL THE LATERAN
PACTS OF 1929.

The two turns taken by the grim reaper are the two world wars of the twentieth century.

The moving sign signifies the movement of the hands of Nostradamus's astrolabe. By turning them in the appropriate manner they indicated on the rim of the instrument the exact numerical sequence that allows a person to chronologically match the quatrains in accordance with an order that literally drew an inclining line, ascending and descending, by using the three ciphers of the numbers of the quatrains. Using these three numbers, for each figure a continuous series of letters emerges, forming the signature of Nostradamus: M. N.

Declaration of the Discovery of the Keys in the Twentieth Century After the Seventh Pope

KEY TEXT: BRANCH XV, 24 QUATRAIN 2 88

It is the circuit of the great ruinous deed
When the name of the seventh is that of the fifth,
When the third, even greater, the warlike stranger
Will take Paris, nor will Provence save her.

È il circuito del gran fatto rovinoso.
Il nome del settimo, del quinto sarà
Del terzo più grande lo straniero bellicoso,
Di quando Parigi in marzo, Provenza non garantirà.

Le circuit du grand faict ruineux,
Au nom septiesme du cinquiesme sera:
D'un tiers plus grand l'estrange belliqueux,
Mouton, Lutece,* Aix ne garentira.

This quatrain bears the key number from which arises the astronomic algorithm responsible for the chronological distribution of the Prophecies: 2 8 8.

The name of the seventh pope of the century would be the same as that of the fifth: John Paul I and John XXIII.

To quote Nostradamus from another quatrain, the great third, the warlike stranger, was the third of "the three brothers, who plunged the world into torment"—the Third Reich. The first two were Stalin and Mussolini. Under the Third Reich Germany would capture Provence, the homeland of Michele Nostradamus.

---

*Lutece was the Latin name for Paris.

Pius XI and the Agreement of 1929

KEY TEXT: BRANCH V, 29 QUATRAIN 10 80

To the great ruler of the grand realm
By force of arms the huge doors of bronze
Shall be made to open by the King and Duke together.
Port demolished, ship foundered, day of light.

Al gran regnante del grande reame
Per forza d'armi le gran porte di rame
Faranno aprire insieme il Re ed il Duce.
Portale demolito, nave alla fonda, giorno di luce.

Au regne grand du grand regnant,
Par force d'armes les grands portes d'airain
Fera ouvrir, le Roy et Duc ioignant,
Port demoly, nef à fons, iour serain.

The Agreement of 1929 put an end to the Vatican imprisonment of the pope. Victor Emanuel III was king, but ruled under the dictatorship of Benito Mussolini, Il Duce of Fascism. Once the wall in front of the Holy See was demolished, the portals of Saint Peter were opened.

KEY TEXT: BRANCH VII, 3 QUATRAIN 5 56

When the venerable Pontiff's hour has come,
A Roman of good age shall be elected
Of whom it will be said that he dishonored his throne
Though he held it long, with virtuous acts.

Del vegliardo Pontefice quando giunto l'ora
Sarà eletto Roman di buona età,
Che si dirà che il Seggio disonora
E invece tiene a lungo con virtuosa attività.

Par le trepas du tres vieillard Pontife
Sera esleu Romain de bon aage,
Qui sera dict que le siege debiffe,
Et long tiendra et de picquant ouvrage.

After the death of Pius XI, Pius XII, Pope Pacelli, was elected. He later would be accused of colluding with the Nazis to deport Jews, when in fact he made every effort to save them.

KEY TEXT: BRANCH VII, 5   QUATRAIN 6 66

After the new pact of arms is sealed,
You will find the bones of the great Roman.
The sepulchre will appear to be covered in marble,
Earthquake in April, inhuman heat.

Al fondamento del nuovo patto d'armi
Trovate l'ossa del grande Romano,
Apparirà il sepolcro rivestito di marmi,
Terremoto in aprile, ardore inumano.

Au fondament de la nouvelle secte,
Seront les os du grand Romain trouvez,
Sepulchre en marbre apparoistra couverte,
Terre trembler en Avril, mal enfouez.

After the Pact of Acciaio, just a few months after his election, Pius XII initiated the excavations that would lead to the rediscovery of the tomb of Saint Peter. The sepulchre was covered in layers of marble from successive rounds of construction. On April 10, 1940, Hitler began his Blitzkrieg.

KEY TEXT: BRANCH VII, 6 QUATRAIN 5 75

He will mount on high to the right of his good
In his dwelling above the square-sided stone,
At midday he will appear at the window,
His curved stick in hand and his iron mouth.

Monterà in alto, del bene più a destra,
Dimora sovrasta la pietra quadrata,
Di mezzogiorno s'affaccia alla finestra,
Baston ritorto in mano, bocca ferrata.

Montera haut sur le bien plus à dextre,
Demourra assis sur la pierre quarree,
Vers le Midy posé à la fenestre,
Baston tortu en main, bouch ferree.

From his palace overlooking the obelisk in the square of Saint Peter (the square-sided stone), to the right of whomever is looking up at him, the Holy Father presents himself at his window at noon. Pius XII carried a crosier with a curved handle and wore a metal prosthetic device in his mouth.

KEY TEXT: BRANCH VII, 7 QUATRAIN 1 92

Though one proclaims peace all around,
Before long comes rebellion and pillage,
For a city's refusal, besieged land and sea,
A third of a million are captured or killed.

Da un la pace ovunque proclamata,
Ma poco dopo sarà piglio e ribellione,
Per rifiuto di città, per terra e mare attaccata,
Morti e prigionieri, il terzo di un milione.

Sous un la paix par tout sera clamee,
Mais non long temps pille et rebellion,
Par refus ville, terre et mer entamme,
Morts et captifs le tiers d'un million.

Pope Pacelli's final, desperate appeal on August 24, 1939, went unheard. Because the Poles refused to surrender Danzig, on the first of September Germany invaded Poland.

PART IV

The Popes

OF THE SECOND HALF OF
THE TWENTIETH CENTURY

The Wheel of Destiny

Yet another confirmation of Nostradamus's machinations exists in the Codex of the seventeenth century. Plates 37 through 53, despite bearing evident traces of the popes of the second half of the twentieth century, reveal some chronological inversions if read in sequence.* It is not that the quatrains are not clear, but that the figures do not follow in temporal, historical sequence.

For example, the two unicorns, both cited in the same quatrain, do not seem to be consecutive. The great shield of Pope Montini, bearing mountains and flowers, appears after the plate of John Paul II, while Pope Paul VI is represented correctly beforehand, and so forth.

As in the quatrains for the Restoration, it follows that this temporal Branch must be ordered not by a straight line but in an undulatory motion, according to the cited technique of dispersing the numbers in an alternately

---

*See Branches XV and XVI of the "Popes of the Twentieth Century" in *The Keys of Nostradamus*.

ascending and descending manner so as to form the initials M. N., completed by points.

> **Insert the moving line in its place,**
> **Equal couples of right inclination.**

Nostradamus is suggesting that the rotation of his astrolabe, used to order the quatrains, united with the "inclinations" of the curve describing the M and the N, will pair the quatrains and the drawings correctly.

The unicorns, then, must be put in order first (Pope John XXIII, followed by Paul VI) to highlight the pacifying function of the "Herald of Peace" with the promulgation of the Second Vatican Council. This is in juxtaposition to the domination by nuclear violence of the large and powerful nations, symbolized by the malevolent unicorns. Not long before, these same powers were conducting diabolical atomic experiments in the equatorial Pacific. By bringing together these known historical events, in a logical manner, with the appropriate figures and the quatrains, the desired graphic M. N. is obtained.

And here is another surprise: By observing the graph of points, one can readily see in its middle a regular hexagon with a round center—a symmetrical design. By bringing the points on the left of center to the right and vice versa, Nostradamus's intent becomes clear: He wished to indicate a wheel with spokes and a scroll underneath. The Wheel of Destiny (see Plate 35) is on his coat of arms, preserved in France in J. B. Rietstap's General Armory, and is cited by Carlo Patrian. On the scroll is his name, Nostradamus. By graphing the points in this way, Nostradamus is actually placing his official stamp on his document.

The correct temporal sequence of the plates in Part IV follows.

SUCCESSIVE PROGRAMMING ON THE COMPUTER RESULTS IN NOSTRADAMUS'S COAT OF ARMS.

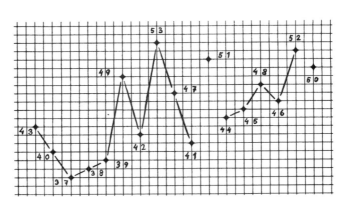

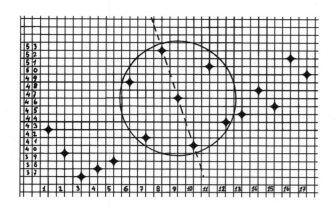

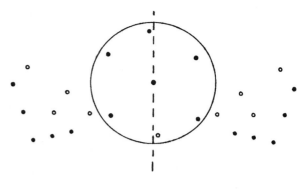

SUCCESSIVE
PROGRAMMING ON THE
COMPUTER RESULTS IN
NOSTRADAMUS'S COAT
OF ARMS.

KEY TEXT: BRANCH XI, 16 QUATRAIN 7 43

When the two unicorns shall be seen,
One rampant, one standing low,
They shall take Borneo, in the middle of the world,
And cause the new irradiant to blaze there.

Quando si vedranno i due unicorni
L'uno abbassato e l'altro abbassante,
Nel mezzo del mondo pigliar Borneo e dintorni
Perchè possa brillar colà nuovo irradiante.

Lors qu'on verra les deux liocornes
L'une baissant, l'autre abaissany,
Monde au milieu, pilier aux Bornes
S'en Luira le neveu Riant.

PLATE 1:43 AND PLATE 2:40 PUT TOGETHER: TWO UNICORNS, ONE RAMPANT, ONE STANDING, WITH CROWN AND SUN.

The United States and Great Britain were the first atomic powers, though the first would outstrip the second. Both are descendants of the unicorn, the heraldic symbol—along with the lion—of the great coat of arms of England.

It was also near Borneo, in the middle of the world (that is, at the equator) that the first atomic experiments were carried out, disseminating lethal radiation throughout the world.

PLATE 3: SAINT FRANCIS OF SALES HANDS SAINT JOAN OF CHANTAL THE RULES OF HER ORDER. AFTERWARDS WILL COME URBAN VIII BARBERINI. THIS ILLUSTRATION CORRESPONDS WITH A PAINTING BY NOEL HALLÉ WHICH HANGS IN THE CHURCH OF SAINT-LOUIS-EN-L'ILE IN PARIS.

PLATE 18: A MONSTROUS KING ABOVE A SEA OF FLAMES. HE WEARS THE PHRYGIAN CAP AND THE EARS OF AN ASS: THE PLEBEIAN SANCULOTTES OF THE FRENCH REVOLUTION TAKE POWER. PIUS VI IS TAKEN PRISONER.

PLATE 23: THE FRENCH REVOLUTION: A KING AND A CLERIC AT THE GUILLOTINE.

PLATE 4:29: HANDS ON THE CITY (1870). THE BREACH OF PORTA PIA. ENTRY OF THE PIEDMONTESE INTO ROME. THE COLUMN ON THE RIGHT COMMEMORATES THE EVENT TWO HUNDRED AND FIFTY YEARS BEFORE IT WAS ACTUALLY PLACED THERE.

PLATE 5:30: A NAKED KING, WITHOUT SOLDIERS (1871). THE POPES LOSE SECULAR POWER. THE POPE IS RECOGNIZABLE BY HIS HAND RAISED IN BLESSING AND HIS TONSURE, AS WELL AS BY THE RESPECTFUL ATTITUDE OF THE CLERIC BESIDE HIM. HE SITS ON A THRONE OF "PIETRO" (PETER) THAT HAS BECOME A SIMPLE "PIETRA" (ROCK).

PLATE 35: THE WHEEL OF DESTINY OF NATIONS AND THE PAPACY. POPE 25 IS SHOWN ON FASCISM'S LEASH. AN EAGLE HOLDING A PAPAL TIARA HOVERS ABOVE A ROUND PLATE AS IN THE COAT OF ARMS. PIUS XI OF DESIO-MILANO, ACHILLE RATTI (1922–1939).

PLATE 3:37: POPE 27 HOLDING THE GLOBE OF THE UNIVERSE WITH LIONS AND FLOWERS ATOP A TOWER. LION, LILIES, AND TOWER APPEAR IN HIS COAT OF ARMS. JOHN XXIII, FROM SOTTO IL MONTE-BERGAMO (1958–1963).

PLATE 4:38: POPE 28 WEARING A CLOAK, RIDING A DRAGON, AND CONFRONTING A BEAR. PAUL VI OF CONCESIO-BRESCIA, GIOVANNI BATTISTA MONTINI (1963–1978). CRISIS OF THE RED BRIGADE: THE YEARS OF LEAD.

PLATE 10:41: AN IMPOSING POPE APPEARS AFTER A MINISCULE POPE, AND A GREAT SUN (DE LABORE SOLIS) REIGNS. THE MADONNA AND CHILD ARE SHOWN IN THE PONTIFF'S CROOK; THEY APPEAR IN HIS COAT OF ARMS AS THE "M" OF MARY WITH THE MOTTO "TOTUS TUUS" (ALL YOURS); JOHN PAUL II IS A POPE DEDICATED TO THE BLESSED VIRGIN. A TURKISH WARRIOR, REPRESENTED WITH HIS SCIMITAR RAISED ON HIGH, DEALS HIM A GRIEVOUS WOUND. IN THE POPE'S HAND IS A BOOK, THE NEW CATECHISM, WITH THREE COINS: FINANCIAL PROBLEMS ARISE DURING HIS REIGN. HE IS EVEN MORE NOTABLE FOR HIS MANY JOURNEYS, SYMBOLIZED BY THE HORSE BEING MAULED BY A LION. A COCK (GALLO), STANDING FOR THE "GALLIC" FRENCH, IS UPPERMOST IN HIS THOUGHTS.

PLATE 12:44: A QUEEN, A FEMALE POPE, AND A SAINTED NUN. THE MADONNA WILL SPEAK TO KINGS, TO POPES, AND TO RELIGIOUS SPIRITS THROUGH CHILDREN.

PLATE 13:45: EEL WITH A WAVY TAIL AND HUMAN FACE, SPRIGS OF GRAIN, A LILY OR HALBERD, A DAGGER IN THE SHAPE OF A CROSS, A CRESCENT MOON, AND A SUN AND STAR.

PLATE 15:46: A FORTRESS IN FLAMES: WAR IN THE EAST.

PLATE 58: A GRYPHON OR DRAGON WITH THE PAPAL CROOK: THE ANTICHRIST.

PLATE 76: A MONK HOLDS A CROOK IN THE SHAPE OF THE CROSS OF LORENA, FRENCH SYMBOL OF THE "FREE FRANCE" OF DE GAULLE IN THE 1940S. HE LEANS ON A STICK, SURROUNDED BY KINGS AND CARDINALS; A POPE SEEMS NOT TO WANT TO ACCEPT THE PONTIFF'S CROOK. POPE JOHN PAUL II, AFTER A FALL, TOOK TO USING A CANE.

PLATE 77: POPE 31 WITH THE CROSS OF LORENA, WHICH IS BEING BURNED BY DESTINY, SYMBOLIZED BY THE DICE AND THE FATAL NUMBER: SIX. THE POPULACE TURNS ITS BACK ON HIM, WHILE WOMEN REACH IN YEARNING FOR HIS CROSS.

PLATE 79: THE CLERGY HACKED TO PIECES. THE POPE ESCAPES FROM THE CITY AND GOES INTO EXILE.

PLATE 81: NEW SEEDS ARE
SOWN, NEW VINES ARE
GROWN: THE NEW
MILLENNIUM.

PLATE 82: THE THREE PARTS OF A HUMAN BEING: BODY, SOUL, AND SPIRIT.

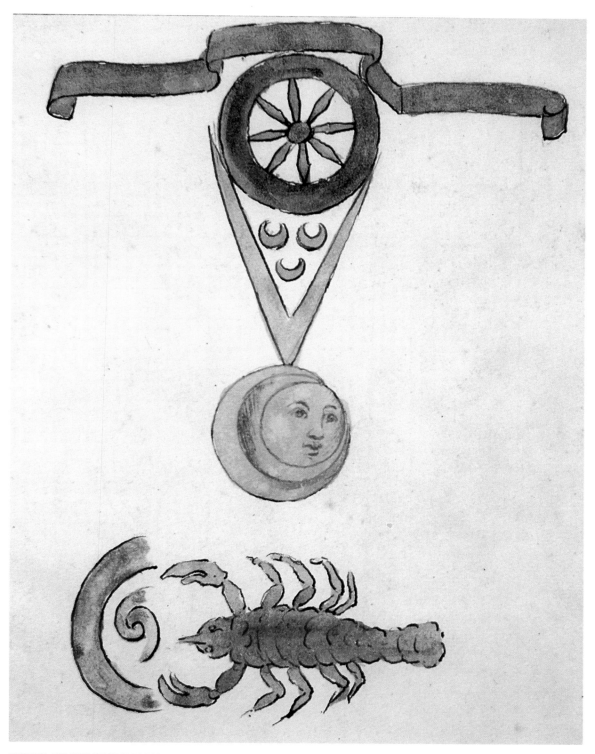

PLATE 70: THE MAN IN THE MOON IS WHAT THE ANCIENTS SAW IN THE MYTH OF ENDYMION—A LOVER OF ALL THINGS OCCULT. THE GREAT MOTHER APPEARS IN GALAXY M51, IN CANES VENATIX UNDER THE SIGN OF CANCER GREAT EVENTS OCCUR IN THE MILKY WAY, IN OUR GALAXY, AND IN OUR SOLAR SYSTEM. THEY LAST FOR THREE CYCLES OF THE MOON. THE GALACTIC SPIRAL IS CLEARLY SHOWN IN THE PICTURE, ALTHOUGH THE GALAXIES WOULD NOT BE DISCOVERED UNTIL THE TWENTIETH CENTURY. THE RIBBON OF STARS AT THE TOP COULD BE THE SYMBOL OF THE MILKY WAY.

PLATE 72: THE MOEBIUS STRIP AT THE TOP SYMBOLIZES THE CYCLE OF ETERNAL RETURN FROM ANOTHER DIMENSION, YET WE ARE SHOWN A WAY OUT: THE SMALL STAR, WHICH IS OUR SPIRITUAL ESSENCE, WILL AT LAST RETURN TO THE GREAT CENTRAL SUN. NOSTRADAMUS GREETS THE FUTURE GENERATIONS AND URGES THEM TO READ HIS BOOK. THE SCROLLS, DRAWN IN PERSPECTIVE, INDICATE HIS EXTENSION INTO TIME TO COME. THE WOMEN ARE WATCHING AND HONORING DIANA, PAGAN GODDESS OF THE HUNT AND THE OCCULT, SYMBOLIZED BY THE DEER.

Plates 37–53: The Popes of the Second Half of the Twentieth Century

V. 1958—John XXIII, *Pastor et Nauta:* reigned five years

VI. 1963—Paul VI, *Flos Florum:* reigned fifteen years

VII. 1978—John Paul I, *De Medietate Lunae*

VIII. 1978—John Paul II, *De Labore Solis*

KEY TEXT: BRANCH XV, 23 PROPHECY 9

To the eighth, the fifteenth, and the fifth, treachery
Will be granted the malignant explorer.
Fear of thunderbolts, fire from heaven, cries to his Holiness,
The West trembles and locks away the wine turned sour.

All'Ottavo, al quindici ed al quinto quale slealtà
Sarà concessa all'esplorator maligno
Per fuoco e folgore dal Ciel paura: clamori a Santità,
Tremante Occidente troppo chiude il vigno asprigno.

Huict, quinze et cinq quelle desloyauté
Viendra permettre l'esplorateur malin.
Feu du Ciel, foudre, peur, frayeur Papauté,
L'Occident tremble, trop serre vin Salin.

HERALDIC CONFIRMATION:
LION, LILIES, TOWER.

John Paul II (the eighth pope of the century), Paul VI (who reigned for fifteen years), and John XXIII (fifth pope of the century with a reign of five years), all experienced torment by betrayals (the Instituto Opere di Religione scandals, the scism of Lefebvre, the Red Brigades, bishops opposing the Vatican Council) and great upheavals such as the end of communism in Russia.

KEY TEXT: BRANCH XV, 6 PROPHECY 7 MAY

Five and six both late and soon for fifteen years adjourn.

The newborn dies in blood, the cities revolt,

From twenty and three the herald of peace returns.

From the open fifth, it is closed with new inventions.

Il cinqe e il sei tardi e tosto per quindicianni aggiorna.
L'appena nato muore, nel sangue di città rivoltate
Dal ventitre di pace araldo se ne torna.
Dal quinto aperto, chiude con novità inventate.

Le cinq, six, quinze, tard et tost l'on se journe.
Le né sang fin: les citez s'en revoltées
L'haraut de paix vint et trois s'en retourne.
L'ouvert cinq serre, nouvelles inventées.

In the drawing we see a pope and the angelic herald of the Universal Council of the Church (globe with keys). The lion and flowers appear on the pope's own coat of arms, as well as on the tower on whose summit he is standing. Instead of a cross at the peak of the papal tiara, we see a lily, this pope's heraldic flower. There are four studs in the tower, representing the four popes of the second half of the twentieth century. (See Plate 66. Under the angel is a UFO, not a cloud as in Plate 33.)

The X on his breast, the crossed keys, and the three crosses on the papal crook form the prophetic number XXIII (indicating Pope John XXIII).

Roncalli promulgated the Second Vatican Council to renew the church and avert the danger of an atomic war. It was an invitation to fraternal union; *Ut unum sint* was the motto of the council.

John XXIII was the fifth pope of the twentieth century.

Paul VI was also the sixth of the series, with a reign of fifteen years. Like his predecessor, he modernized the papacy with the Second Vatican Council.

After Paul VI, the new pope John Paul I died during the course of the Red Brigades's attack on the State in 1978. A herald of peace, he returned to heaven, bearing the same name as his predecessor John XXIII.

The works of the Vatican Council were shut down in 1965. One of its most controversial changes was the abolition of the Latin Mass.

KEY TEXT: BRANCH XVI, 12 QUATRAIN 8 16

Where Geryon had his ship built
There will be a flood so sudden and great
That no earth or resting place will be seen.
The waves will mount up to Olympian Fiesole.

Dove Gerione fece sua nave fabbricare
Sarà un diluvio così improvviso e grande
Che non si vede luogo né terra ove posare,
al Fiesolano Olimpico monteranno le onde.

Au lieu que ieron feit sa nef fabriquer
Si grande deluge sera et si subite
Qu'on n'aura lieu ne terres s'ataquer,
L'onde monter Fesulan Olympique.

In the *Fiesole of the Olympic* hillside suburb of Rome, overlooking the city as Fiesole overlooks Florence, is the Via Fani, far above the Via Olympic and Olympic stadium of Rome, the same place Aldo Moro was kidnapped and his escort murdered. The future promises more gravely subversive events like this in Rome.

Geryon, a mythical monster (see Plate 4:38), was a symbol of the fraudulent (see Dante's *Inferno,* Canto XVII). The fraudulent are the governments (the ships) of the corrupt political parties who, like the Christian Democrats, desire the pope's help.

KEY TEXT: BRANCH XVI, 5 QUATRAIN 4 11

He who will go covered in a great cape
Will be lead to plead someone's cause:
A dozen red ones will come to stain the cloth,
For death, more death will be dealt.

Colui che andrà coperto da gran cappa
Sarà indotto qualche causa a perorare
Di rossi una dozzina verrà a macchiare il drappo
Per morte altra morte si verrà perpetrare.

Celuy qu'aura couvert de la grand cappe,
Sera induict à quelque cas patrer:
Les douze rouges viendront souiller la nappe
Soubs meurtre, meurtre se viendra perpetrer.

In the illustration we see a warrior pope, wrapped in his cape and battling a terrible bear.

PLATE 4:38: POPE 28, DRESSED IN A CAPE, RIDES A DRAGON AND CONFRONTS A BEAR. (SEE COLOR PLATE 4:38.)

PAUL VI OF CONCESIO-BRESCIA, GIOVANNI BATTISTA MONTINI (1963–78), WHO SUFFERED THE CRISES OF THE RED BRIGADES AND THE YEARS OF LEAD.

PROPHETIC NAME: *FLOS FLORUM* (FLOWER AMONG FLOWERS).

KEY TEXT: BRANCH XVI, 29 QUATRAIN 8 19

He who bears the great cape will be troubled
By grave scandal as the reds march on,
The family of the dead man will be almost prostrate
But reds to reds add more red still.

A sostener la gran cappa turbata
Dal grave scandalo i rossi marceranno,
Del morto la famiglia sarà quasi prostrata
Ma i rossi ai rossi, il rosso aggiungeranno.

A soutenir la grand cappe troublee,
Pour l'esclaircir les rouges marcheront,
De mort famille sera presque accablee,
Les rouges les rouges rouge assommeront.

In 1978, Pope Paul VI Montini took on the defense of the kidnapped president of the Christian Democrats, Aldo Moro. In the end, the Red Brigades were defeated and reason restored, but only after the death of both hostage and pope.

KEY TEXT: BRANCH XVI, 21 QUATRAIN 8 18

The exit of Flora will be the cause of his death
Hatched over time in plots both old and new,
Such is the fate to befall the three lilies
For their mistaken fruit and their rotten pulp.

L'uscita di Flora sarà causa di sua morte
Fra qualche tempo per nuova e vecchia trama ordita
Per i tre gigli gli faranno aver tal sorte
Per il lor frutto sbagliato, dalla polpa marcita.

De Flore issue de sa mort sera cause,
Un temps devant par ieusne et vielle bueyre
Par les trois lys luy feront telle pause,
Par son fruit fauve comme chair crue mueyre.

Plate 5:39 clearly illustrates the following concept: The flock attacked by a lion with three lilies in his mouth symbolizes the mistaken fruits of the Second Vatican Council, and the renewal initiated by the pope with the lion and lilies on his crest (John XXIII), cut down too early by another "flower among flowers" (Paul VI). His invocation to the men of the Red Brigades and his subsequent delusion—"God, you have not been pleased to listen to me"—caused great trauma in the pontiff's spirit and he died, not of illness, but from the exhaustion of his trials. The three lilies symbolize a pure and generous youth led astray by mad ideologies.

KEY TEXT: BRANCH XVI,
19 PROPHECY 8 18 OCTOBER

Rain and wind, the hour of the hysterical barbaric band
    has come.
Supplies, munitions, and soldiers pass through Tyrrhenia,
Cross over Siena, reduce the successes of FLORA.
The two will be killed, united in friendship.

HERALDIC CONFIRMATION: LION AND LILIES ON THE CREST OF JOHN XXIII. THREE LILIES AND SMALL MOUNTAINS (*MONTINI*) ON THE CREST OF PAUL VI. FROM THE LION OF SAINT MARK WILL SPRING THE THREE LILIES OF POPE MONTINI.

Pioggia e vento, di Barbara Isterica banda giunge l'ora.
Rifornimenti, munizioni e soldati passare al Tirreno.
Ribelli i suoi, ridotti i successi di FLORA,
Dall'amicizia uniti i due, giunti al momento estremo.

Pluy, vent, classe Barbare Ister. Tyrrhene
Passer holbades Ceres, soldats munies.
Reduits bienfaits par FLOR, franchie Siene.
Les deux seront morts, amitiez unies.

Barbara Balzarani, the noted exponent of the Red Brigade, was condemned to life imprisonment and sentenced in the first degree. "Holbades" equals "halebarde," that is, gendarmes. FLORA is Pope Paul VI, the *Flos Florum* of the prophecies. Both he and his friend Aldo Moro died in 1978.

PLATE 6:49: MOUNTAINS AND FLOWERS: THE *FLOS FLORUM* OF THE SECOND VATICAN COUNCIL.

HERALDIC CONFIRMATION: MOUNTAINS AND FLOWERS ON THE CREST OF PAUL VI.

KEY TEXT: BRANCH XVI, 20 QUATRAIN 6 52

Where the great man comes to be put to death,
Unimprisoned, his loyal friend stands in his square:
After six months the Trojan hope will die stillborn.
When the Sun is elected, ice fills the rivers.

Dove il grande verrà messo a morte
Fuor di prigione, nella sua piazza l'amico leale:
A sei mesi giunta troiana speranza avrà stessa sorte.
Il Sol quando eletto, i fiumi riempiti di gelo invernale.

En lieu du grand qui sera condanné,
De prison hors, son amy en sa place:
L'espoir Troyen en six mois ioins mort né,
Le Sol à l'urne seront peins fleuve en glace.

In both the Via Caetani and the Square of Saint Peter in Rome, Pope Paul VI pleaded publicly for the Red Brigades to liberate his friend Aldo Moro. The "Trojan hope" of finding an historic compromise by entering the enemy camp, as with Troy's wooden horse, died stillborn. When the "Sun"—John Paul II, the *De Labore Solis*—was elected, the course of politics with the Communist Left was frozen until the collapse of the Soviet Union. The Center Left predicted by Moro would come into being seventeen years later in 1995 with the agreement between the Populist Party and the Democratic Party of the Left (the PDS).

KEY TEXT: BRANCH XVI, 25 QUATRAIN 7 08

Flora passed on, the next Roman will pass on as well,
To the Fiesolan will be given great conflict:
Blood shed and a hand laid over the great ones,
Neither temple nor sex shall be pardoned.

Flora passato, passerà anche il prossimo Romano
Al Fiesolano il conflitto capitato
Sangue sparso, sopra i grandi messa la mano
Né al tempio né al sesso sarà perdonato.

Flora, fuis, fuis le plus proche Romain,
Au Fesulan sera conflict donné:
Sang espandu, les plus grands prins à main,
Temple ne sexe ne sera pardonné.

KEY TEXT: BRANCH XV 1 QUATRAIN 6 13

A doubtful one will not reign long,
The greater part will wish to help him,
A capitol will stand against him.
He will fail to bring his great work to fruition.

Un dubitoso non resta troppo al regno,
La maggior parte lo vorrà aiutare,
Però un capitolo sarà contro il suo regno.
Suo grande incarico non potrà terminare.

Un dubiteux ne viendra loing du regne,
La plus grand part le voudra soustenir,
Un capitole ne voudra pas qu'il regne,
Sa grande charge ne pourra maintenir.

We see in Plate 7:42 the shields of Montini (the mountains) and Roncalli (the Lion of Saint Mark), but the creature's raised paw, which in Roncalli's coat of arms holds the book of the Gospel of Saint Mark, is here leaning on empty air: *The Book of the Vatican Council* would not be completed by him, but by Montini. Elderly and isolated, Pope Roncalli doubted his own ability to renew the Church, a renewal he felt to be urgent. For this reason he called together the Second Vatican Council, which he could not bring to completion, and the labors of the council ended in 1965. One of its most controversial innovations was the abolition of the Latin Mass, an innovation opposed by the traditionalist Cardinal Lefebvre, who continued to ordain priests in the ancient way.

KEY TEXT: BRANCH XIX, 4 QUATRAIN 6 82

In the deserts of a place both free and fierce
The successor of the great pope will come to wander
Together with the descendants of that atrocious stock
Who, when the year adds up to seven, will occupy Cyprus.

Pei deserti di luogo libero e feroce
Verrà errare del gran papa il successore
Insieme ai discendenti di quel ceppo atroce
Che, sommato a sette l'anno, è di Cipro occupatore.

Par les deserts de lieu libre et farouche,
Viendra errer nepveu du grand Pontife:
Assomé à sept avecques lourde souche,
Par ceus qu'apres occuperont le Cyphe.

Pope Paul VI's journey to the Holy Land preceded the war of Sinai and the occupation of Cyprus. Golgotha, or Calvary (also known as the Mount of Skulls and the place Jesus was crucified) is used as a symbol of a land without peace that, in the time of Paul VI, relied on the United Nations forces.

HERALDIC CONFIRMATION:
THE LION ON JOHN XXIII'S
COAT OF ARMS AND THE
MOUNTAINS ON PAUL VI'S
SHIELD.

Skirmishes and conflicts between East and West, symbolized by the crescent moon atop the skull, are well delineated in the quatrains: the Turkish occupation of Cyprus, the interventions of the UN, the slaughter in the refugee camps. The journey of the pope is alluded to by the tiara's ribbons fluttering under the skull.

Paul VI, Pope John XXIII's successor, traveled in relative peace to the Holy Land in May of 1964. Less peaceful were the peregrinations of the Arabs in the Negev and Sinai deserts during the 1967 Arab-Israeli War. Cyprus was first occupied by the Turks in 1571, seven years after the year of the pope's journey, though four centuries before. At that time, after a strenuous resistance but the ultimate surrender of the stronghold of Famagosta, the Venetian commander Marcantonio Bragadin was flayed alive and all his

PLATE 8:53: CRESCENT MOON, SKULL, AND CRUTCH ON A MOUNTAIN, WITH THE SHADOW OF A DEER IN THE ROCK (GERMANY AND THE THIRD REICH). IN 1964 POPE PAUL VI JOURNEYED TO ISRAEL—GOLGOTHA AND SINAI. GOLGOTHA IS THE MOUNT OF THE SKULL. THE CRUTCH MOST LIKELY PREDICTS A FUTURE JOURNEY ON THE PART OF JOHN PAUL II WHO, BECAUSE OF A BONE FRACTURE, NEEDED TO USE A CANE.

soldiers run through with swords. In 1974 Famagosta was occupied for the second time when the Greek Cypriots became divided by the line of Attila from the Turkish Cypriots who disembarked to oppose the *Enosis* (annexation) threatened by the Greek colonels. In the camps of Sabra and Chatila, the families of the absent guerrilla fighters were ruthlessly massacred and thrown into a common grave. Israel refused to take responsibility for the act.

KEY TEXT: BRANCH XIX, 18 QUATRAIN 8 55

Between two rivers you will see the besieged,
In armored cars the united peacekeeping troops will pass
Eight bridges to the broken chief and many enclosed there.
Perfect children will be slaughtered as they lie in their
    blankets.

Entro due fiumi si vedrà assediato,
Carri armati i caschi uniti passeranno
Otto ponti, in rotta il capo, ai tanti recintati,
Ragazzi per fatti, fra le coltri sgozzati saranno.

Entre deux fleuves se verra enserré,
Tonneaux et caques unis à passer outre,
Huict ponts rompus chef a tant enserré
Enfans parfaicts son iugules en oultre.

In 1982 Yassir Arafat, the chief of the PLO, abandoned Lebanon and left it to the protection of the *caschi blu,* the United Nation's peacekeeping troops.

KEY TEXT: BRANCH XIX, 19 PROPHECY 11 34

Princes and Lords will all go to war,
German cousins and brother with brother.
The Bourbon heir's arbitration is over,
Jerusalem's princes, so easy to love,
For enormous and execrable deeds committed
Withdraw from the lip of the unending chasm.

Principi e Signori tutti verranno alle armi,
Fratello col fratello e coi cugini germani,
Finito l'arbitrato dell'erede del Borbone,
I principi di Gerusalemme tanto amabili,
Dei fatti commessi enormi ed esecrabili,
Si ritrarranno dall'orribile burrone.

Princes et Seigneurs tous se feront la guerre,
Cousin Germain, le frere avec le frere,
Finy l'Arby de l'heureux de Bourbon.
De Hierusalem les Princes tant aymables,
Du fait commis enormes et execrable,
Se ressentiront sur la bourse sans fond.

KEY TEXT: BRANCH XV, 13 QUATRAIN 10 12

Elected Pope, his election is mocked,
Provoking sudden strong emotion in this timid man.
Too much goodness and sweetness lead him to death,
A gentle guide extinguished on the night he departs.

Eletto Papa, de'elezion sarà beffato,
Subita improvvisa emozione, da timido ardita,
Per troppa bontà e dolcezza a morte provocato,
Timorosa guida estinta la notte di sua dipartita.

Esleu en Pape, d'esleu sera mocqué,
Subit soudain esmeu prompt et timide,
Par trop bon doux à mourir provoqué,
Crainte estainte la nuict de sa mort guide.

In this illustration, a pope is elected by angels. Before the conclave lies a strong horse-king, clear reference to the imminent succession by the forceful Pope John Paul II. It is probable that Pope Luciani discovered a financial scam in the Vatican and that the shock of this discovery led to his death. His successor, however, did not share his sensitivities.

KEY TEXT: BRANCH XVI, 2 PROPHECY 54 SEPTEMBER

The Arabs shall be deprived of their weapons:
Their greatest quarrels shall increase.
Thunderstruck Albino, generous Father,
Seven corrosives will strike to the marrow.

Privati saran l'Arabi dell'arme
Aumenteran loro proteste e allarme
Albino folgorato, Padre generoso
Fino al midollo saran sette corrose.

Privez seront Razes de Leur Harnois:
Augmentera leur plus grande querelle,
Pere Liber deceu fulg. Albanois. [SIC]
Seront rongées sectes à la moelle.

KEY TEXT: BRANCH XV, 3 QUATRAIN 6 06

It will come by way of the West
Not far from the shooting comet of Cancer.
In Italy barbaric madness runs rampant.
In Rome the great one is dead and the night is stealing away.

Giungerà da settentrionale via
Non lungi da luglio cometa fuggente,
Corre in Italia barbarica follia
Morir di Roma il grande, la notte scomparente.

Apparoistra vers le Septentrion,
Non loin de Cancer l'estoille chevelue,
Suze, Sienne, Boece, Eretrion,
Mourra de Rome grand, la nuict disparue.

KEY TEXT: BRANCH XV, 7 QUATRAIN 5 83

Those who will undertake to subvert
The reign of equal name, invincible and powerful
By night, by fraud, will cause all three to fail,
The greatest at his bench, reading in his Bible.

Quelli che avranno intrapreso a sovvertire
Uguale nome regna, invincibile e possente:
Faran per frode di notte alle tre fallire,
Al banco il piu grande la Bibbia leggente.

Ceux qui auront entreprins subvertir
Nom pareil regne, puissant et invincible:
Feront par fraude, nuicts trois advertir,
Quant le plus grand à table lira Bible.

In 1978 the Palestinians were forced to surrender to their armed enemies. It was the time of *De Medietate Lunae*, the lunar interval of John Paul I, Albino Luciani, whose light was like a streaking comet. The ways and means of his death correspond to events described in the above quatrains, although a clear complicitous plot was never uncovered.

KEY TEXT: BRANCH XV, 26 QUATRAIN 8 69

After the old angel gives way to the young
Who will come to surpass him in the end,
Ten years passed and restored to the oldest,
Of three, two ready for death, the eighth a seraph.

Dopo che il giovane l'angel vecchio abbassare,
E lo verrà superare alla fine:
Diecianni trascorsi al più vecchio vien ridare,
Dei tre, due morti un resta, l'ottavo serafino.

Aupres du ieune le vieux ange baisser,
Et le viendra surmonter à la fin:
Dix ans esgaux aux plus vieux rabaisser,
De trois deux l'un huictiesme seraphin.

The reign of Pope John XXIII (the old angel) lasted ten years less than that of Pope Paul VI. Of the three popes in 1978, John Paul II, the successor of John Paul I, was eighth in the series of twentieth-century popes. The horse of the traveling pope, being mauled by the lion of the pope of the council, John XXIII, may signify that the following of that assembly would not be persecuted. As depicted in the illustration, a Turkish terrorist, Ali Agca, made an attempt on the life of the pope.

PLATE 10:41: AN IMPOSING POPE APPEARS AFTER A MINISCULE POPE AND A GREAT SUN (*DE LABORE SOLIS*) REIGNS. THE MADONNA AND CHILD DEPICTED IN THE POPE'S CROOK CORRESPOND TO THE M OF MARY IN HIS COAT OF ARMS WITH THE MOTTO *TOTUS TUUS* (ALL YOURS); JOHN PAUL II IS DEDICATED TO THE BLESSED VIRGIN. THE TURKISH WARRIOR SHOWN WITH HIS SCIMITAR RAISED DEALS THE POPE A GRIEVOUS WOUND. IN THE POPE'S HAND IS A BOOK, THE NEW CATECHISM, WITH THREE COINS: FINANCIAL PROBLEMS ARISE DURING HIS REIGN. HE IS EVEN MORE NOTED FOR HIS MANY JOURNEYS, SYMBOLIZED BY THE HORSE BEING MAULED BY THE LION. A COCK (*GALLO*), STANDING FOR THE *GALLIC* FRENCH, IS UPPERMOST IN HIS THOUGHTS. (SEE COLOR PLATE 10:41.)

HERALDIC CONFIRMATION: THE M OF MARY IN THE LOWER RIGHT OF THE POPE'S SHIELD.

KEY TEXT: BRANCH XV, 16 QUATRAIN 2 97

Roman Pontiff you must not approach

The city that reddens two rivers.

It is there one will come to spill your blood,

Yours and your beloveds' when the red rose blooms.

PLATE 11:51:
PAPAL TIARA AND A FIST
HOLDING A ROSE: THE
ASSASSINATION ATTEMPT
IN SAINT PETER'S SQUARE
ON MAY 13, 1981.

Roman Pontefice non ti devi avvicinare
A quella città che due acque arrossa,
Verrà di là chi il tuo sangue versare,
Tuo e dei tuoi, quando fiorirà la rosa rossa.

Romain Pontife garde de t'approcher,
De la cité que deux fleuves arrouse,
Ton sang viendra aupres de là cracher,
Toy et les tiens quand fleurira la rose.

In 1981 the political party of the French Socialists, touting the symbol of a rose in a fist and taken up in Italy by the radicals of Pannella, succeeded in handing over power to President Mitterrand. The Turk Ali Agca escaped from the prison in Constantinople where he was being held for the homicide of a journalist and managed to reach the Square of Saint Peter in Rome, where he wounded the pope in the belly, as well as wounding those who were with him. In 1979 the pope visited the city of two rivers (the Bosphorus and the Horn of Gold)—reddened by bloodthirsty sultans—in a vain attempt to reconcile the two faiths. This provoked the ire of the Grey Wolves of Agca who were already threatening him at the time.

KEY TEXT: BRANCH XV, 19 QUATRAIN 2 98

He who washes his face in the blood
Of the nearby sacrificed victim,
Returning in August, as the auger foretold,
Is then put to death for his faith.

Colui che si deterge il viso
Dal sangue della vittima vicin sacrificata,
Di tornare ad agosto l'augurio e di presagio avviso,
A morte condannato allor per la sua fede.

Celuy du sang reperse le visage,
De la victime proche sacrificée,
Tonant en Leo, augure par presage,
Mis estre à mort lors pour la fiancee.

In August 1993 the pope returned to the Gemelli Clinic for an operation, due to the wound he sustained during Agca's assassination attempt.

KEY TEXT: BRANCH XV, 10 QUATRAIN 4 24

On earth the sainted voice of the Holy Lady is heard,
Human flame for divine will be seen to shine:
It will cause Sisters' blood to be shed on the ground,
Sacred temples cast into ruin by the impure of heart.

In terra udita santa voce della Dama santa,
Ma umana fiamma si vedrà brillare per divina
Farà delle sorelle, di lor sangue terra spanta
E i sacri templi per gli impuri alla rovina.

Ouy soubs terre saincte Dame voix sainte,
Humane flamme pour divine voir luire:
Fera des seuls de leur sang terre tainte,
Et les sainctes temples pour les impurs destruire.

According to the prediction of the Third Message of Fatima, the Madonna will speak through kings, popes, and women of religion until peace comes to humanity. Since 1981 She has appeared in Medjugorje, Bosnia, to three young girls, as well as to others among the faithful, and in its devotion the populace has raised a great church to Her there. But Her voice has been drowned out by the clashing of weapons, and antireligious sentiment has caused many Catholic nuns to be violated and murdered in the name of ethnic cleansing. No one stops to consider that Her miraculous appearance may have been a prophetic invitation for peace just before the former Yugoslavia became a bloody battleground.

From Nostradamus's Prophecy 10 (Branch XIV, 27):

> Six, douze, treize, vint parlera la Dame. (Six, twelve, thirteen, twenty the Lady will speak.)

Note that the four most important apparitions occurred on the following dates:

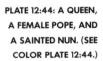

PLATE 12:44: A QUEEN, A FEMALE POPE, AND A SAINTED NUN. (SEE COLOR PLATE 12:44.)

February 6, 1850 at Lourdes (Tarbes)
April 12, 1947 at the Three Fountains (Rome)
May 13, 1917 at Fatima (Santarem)
June 24, 1981 at Medjugorje (Mostar)

Pope John Paul II, whose shield bears the M of Mary, also made pilgrimage to the grotto of Lourdes on August 15, 1983. This pilgrimage led to the discovery of the keys of order, in that the two following quatrains were confirmed at that time in such a way as to reveal their connection by a numerical algorithm. Extraordinarily, I was reading them that very day and was so profoundly impressed that I took up the study of the logic behind the ordering of the quatrains.

KEY TEXT: BRANCH XV, 17 QUATRAIN 6 01

Surrounded by the Pyrenees Mountains, a great crowd
Of foreign peoples follow the newmade king
By the River Garonne to the mountain's great temple,
When the shy Roman patriarch walks to the water.

Attorno ai monti Pirenei gran massa
Di gente straniera seguir nuovo monarca
Presso la Garonna al gran tempio del monte passa
La temerà nell'acqua il Roman patriarca.

Autour des monts Pyrennees grans amas
De gent estrange secourir Roy nouveau
Pres de Garonne du grand Temple du Mas
Un Romain chef le craindra dedans l'eau.

KEY TEXT: BRANCH XV, 20 QUATRAIN 10 29

Solar man from Polonia, seized as he entered
The goatherder's cavern, pulled forth by the beard,
Overseen like some low beast,
Is taken across the Pegourdans to Tarbes.

Uomo solar da Polonia in caverna caprina

Entrato e preso, fuori estratto per la barba

Sorvegliato come bestia mastina

Attraverso i Pegourdans portato a Tarbe.

De pol mansol dans caverne caprine

Caché et prins extrait hors par la barbe,

Captif mené comme beste mastine

Par Pegourdans amenee pres de Tarbe.

In August of 1983, Pope John Paul II, *De Labore Solis,* journeyed to Tarbes (specifically mentioned in the quatrain), the central town of Lourdes, to thank the Blessed Virgin for having saved him from the assassination attempt on his life. From the temple built centuries after the prophecy was written, surrounded by the crowd, and accompanied by President Mitterand, John Paul II walked to the miraculous spring in the cavern where Bernadette tended her goats. In that the pope came from Polonia, it could be said that a "barbarian"* had ascended to the papacy. After his attempted murder he was placed under the strictest surveillance. He was always shy, timid with crowds.

KEY TEXT: BRANCH XX, 16 QUATRAIN 3 21

At Sabino Sabatino on the Adriatic shore

There will appear a strange eel

With human face, but with his tail in the wave

That will be taken using neither hook nor harpoon.[†]

Al Crustamin, da Adriatica sponda

Apparirà uno strano capitano,

Di faccia umana, ma con la coda nell'onda

Che si prenderà senza usar amo né arpione.

---

*Translator's note: The word "barbarian," loosely used in Europe in Nostradamus's time to mean any foreigner, stems from the Latin (and Italian) word "barba," or beard.

[†]Translator's note: The above quatrain is the English translation of Mr. Ramotti's Italian quatrain, which differs in some details from the French. Following find my literal translation of the original:

> *At Crustamin on the Adriatic Sea*
> *There will appear a horrible fish*
> *With human face and acquatic tail,*
> *That will be taken without a fishhook.*

Au Crustamin par mer Hadriatique,
Apparoistra un horrible poisson,
De face humaines et la fin aquatique,
Qui se prendra dehors de l'amecon.

In this picture (Plate 13:45), published by Enza Massa in the *Giornale dei Misteri (Journal of Mysteries)* in March 1987, there appears an ironically metaphoric image of the Roman translator who comes from Trieste on the Adriatic Sea and lives in the Crustumerium, (the Roman countryside) at Anguillara Sabazia on Lake Sabatino. Recently, the very ancient "Crustamin" or "Crutumerium," the grainary in the time of Romulus, has been precisely identified as Settebagni, located on the consular road Salaria, which comes from the Adriatic Sea. Selt cloagni lies just outside the boundaries of Rome.

PLATE 13:45: AN EEL WITH A WAVY TAIL AND HUMAN FACE, SPRIGS OF GRAIN, A LILY OR HALBERD, A DAGGER IN THE SHAPE OF A CROSS, A CRESCENT MOON, AND A SUN AND STAR. (SEE COLOR PLATE 13:45.)

Massa's prophecies were published in the time of conflict between East and West in 1990 that led to the Gulf War in 1991, and Massa was caught between the cross and the crescent moon as depicted in the plate. In 1987 the first edition of my book *The Keys of Nostradamus* was also published—a possible reference to this image?

Other telling symbols are the sprigs of grain from the Roman countryside, one of which is shaped like a lilied halberd as in the coat of arms of Trieste; the sinusoidal form that suggests the undulatory method of ordering the quatrains; and the aquatic creature *(anguilla)* for Anguillara, the town in which I live, is named. The lily appears again as a watermark in the manuscript. And the *Giornale dei Misteri* is published in Florence. According to the prediction, these translations "will flower in Florence." Indeed, although its editor is Roman, the book was curiously enough published in Florence under the sign of the lily of the Valois and the Medici, Nostradamus's kings.

The alchemical Sun of prophetic clarity and the star that my friend and fellow Nostradamus scholar Giancarlo Rossi suggests may be the symbol of NATO—the compass rose—is positioned near the Western dagger. Mr. Rossi also encouraged me to track down the manuscript with the other illustrations, which is how we came to find that Sun of clarity: eighty ancient prophetic illustrations of all the popes to come, according to predictions lost in the mist of time, written before the great renewal of the Church.

The popes of the twentieth century were fully identifiable in the quatrains published in my previous book *The Keys of Nostradamus,* thus I was able to check many details in them that coincided with the symbols present in the prophetic images. This double verification augments the prophetic force of both quatrains and paintings chronologically ordered. As mentioned, in some parts even the pages actually follow the sinusoidal progression M N (Michele Nostradamus), furnishing us with a final confirmation of this system of temporal order.

KEY TEXT: BRANCH XXI, 30 QUATRAIN 5 39

Sprung from the true branch of the fleur de lys
The Etrurian heir is set down, given lodging:
His ancient blood by a long hand plotted,
He will make Florence flower in her own arms' sign.

Dal vero ramo del fiordaliso uscito
Messo e installato d'Etruria ereditiere:
Suo sangue antico da lunga mano ordito,
Farà fiorir Fiorenza sotto uguali araldiche bandiere.

Du vray rameau de fleur de lys yssu
Mis et logé heritier d'Hetrurie:
Son sang antique de longue main tissu,
Fera Florence florir en l'Armoire.

KEY TEXT: BRANCH XVI, 4 QUATRAIN 9 74

In the city of Fert sadistic murder
Done and crimes, great bulls sent to the slaughter,
Once again they return to the rites of Diana
And bury dead bodies for Vulcan.

Nella città di Fert sadica fama
Fatti e misfatti, gran tori andran mattare
Ancor si torna ad onorare Diana
E per Vulcano corpi morti ad affossare.

Dans la cité de Fert sod homicide
Fait et fait multe beuf arant ne macter,
Retour encores aux honeurs d'Artemide,
Et à Vulcan corps morts sepulturer.

After the white magic of the Divine Letters comes black magic. Fert is the motto of the House of Savoy, as Turin and Rome were the capitals of the former Kingdom of Italy. The word "sadism" is derived from the Marquis De Sade, who was infamous during the 1700s for his enjoyment of torture. This is a significant anachronism used to indicate a taste for diabolic rites and sacrifices. Many people in Turin and Rome still honor the pagan gods of violence; Turin especially has become the capital city of black magic, housing the largest number of priests performing actual exorcisms.

PLATE 14:48: A BULL
(*TORO*), SYMBOL OF
TURIN (*TORINO*), AND THE
MOON, SYMBOL OF THE
LUNAR GODDESS OF THE
OCCULT, ARTEMIS TO THE
GREEKS AND DIANA TO
THE ROMANS.

KEY TEXT: BRANCH I/MILLENIUM, 1 PROPHECY 8

When the wandering herald of the dog returns to the Lion
Fire will burn in the city, pillaged and taken anew.
Ships will appear. Prisoners return to their princes.
French diplomats taken. To the great one the damsel is joined.

Quando l'araldo errante—il cane della Luna—al Leone
*   torna*
Fuoco arderà la città saccheggio e presa novella.
Apparire le navi. Ai principi i prigionieri restituti.
Diplomatici presi di Francia. Al grande unita pulzella.

L'heraut errant du chien au Lion tourne.
Feu ardra ville, pille, prise nouvelle.
Decouvrir fustes. Princes pris. on retourne.
Explor. Pris Gall. Au grand jointe pucelle.

PLATE 15:46: A FORTRESS
IN FLAMES. (SEE COLOR
PLATE 15:46.)

Once again we see the lunar influence, this time Islamic. During the Gulf
War a chain of fires marked the withdrawal of Saddam from Kuwait.

Chien: In the Orient, Venus is called the dog or herald of the moon because
it precedes the moon's appearance in the evening. It is present in the form of
a star next to the crescent moon on many Islamic standards. When Venus
approached the Lion (August 2, 1990) Saddam Hussein took Kuwait. Venus
enters Leo on the thirteenth of August.

Pille: The looting of rich Kuwaiti stores by the invading troops.

Prise nouvelle: Invasion of a new kind. Until 1991, this coast of the Gulf had
been spared the war.

Fustes: The United States launched war ships immediately to the Gulf. The
fustes were small Oriental galleys. The term is used to identify the theater of
operations.

Princes: Many hostages from other nations were returned to their countries.

Explor.: From the Latin explorator, or military spy. Using the excuse that it feared military spies, Iraq treated Westerners as hostages.

Pucelle: Maiden or damsel. In the figurative lexicon of Nostradamus, *Pucelle* signifies a small nation, while the word *Dame* stands for a larger one. A small nation, therefore, is being forced to unite with a powerful one (grand).

KEY TEXT: BRANCH II/MILLENIUM, 16 QUATRAIN 4 66

Under the false guise of faith of the shaved heads
Many saboteurs shall be sown,
Watering the wells and the fountains with poison,
Human devourers of the strength of the West.*

Sotto l'aspetto finto di fede di teste rasate
Saranno seminati molti sabotatori
Di pozzi e fontane del veleno innaffiati
Dei forti d'Occidente, uman consumatori.

Sous couleur fainte de sept testes rasees,
Seront semez divers explorateurs,
Puits et fontains de poisons arrousees.
Au fort de Gennes humains devorateurs.

The shaved heads symbolize the Mohammedans.

This quatrain refers to the arson of the oil wells in Kuwait. Seeing that he had lost the war, Saddam Hussein sought to damage the West in the name of the Holy War of Islam by setting fire to more than five hundred oil wells he was being forced to abandon. The fires burned a long time, contaminating the entire region for months.

KEY TEXT: BRANCH II/MILLENNIUM, 19 QUATRAIN 2 64

The folk of the West are dried up with hunger and thirst,
Their next hope will fall into failure.
The moment reached, Geneva's law will vacillate,
The fleet at the great port will gather up little.

---

*Translator's note: A literal translation from the French of the first line reads: Under the faint color of seven shaved heads.

Di fame dimagrita e di sete la gente d'Occidente
La prossima speranza verrà al fallimento
Giunti al momento, oscillante sara legge ginevrina
Flotta al gran porto si può poca raccogliere.

Seicher de faim, de soif, gent Genevoise,
Espoir prochain viendra au deffaillir,
Sur point tremblant sera loy Gebenoise,
Classe au grand port ne se peu acueillir.

After the Gulf War, the next intervention of the United Nation's peacekeeping troops was much less prompt in the former Yugoslavia. For years a cruel war dragged on in Sarajevo and all of Bosnia, always under the influence of the Islamic crescent moon.

PLATE 16:52: THE YEAR 1991. THE LILIES OF FRANCE DISTANCE THEMSELVES FROM THE HEART. A TURTLE IS SLOWLY GOING ALONG. AN IRON CROWN IMPOSES ITS POWER. THE TURTLE SYMBOLIZES THE SLOWNESS AND HESITATION OF THE WEST.

KEY TEXT: BRANCH III/MILLENNIUM, 12 QUATRAIN 4 55

When the crow climbs atop the tower of bricks
For seven hours he will do nothing but scream:
Augering death for the blood-tainted statue,
Death for the tyrant, as the people turn to God.

Quando il corvo sulla torre di mattoni sale
Durante sette ore non farà che gridare:
Morte presagisce di statua di rosso sangue tinta
Morto il tiranno, a Dio il popolo si volge.

Quand la corneille sur tour de brique ioincte,
Durant sept heures ne fera que crier:
Mort presagee de sang statue taincte,
Tyran meurtry, aux Dieux peuple prier.

Boris Yeltsin, known as the White Crow, first climbed the tower of an armored car and then the tower of Parliament to take power. Statues of Lenin were knocked down and the orthodox clergy regained its influence in Russia.

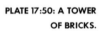

PLATE 17:50: A TOWER OF BRICKS.

PART V

The Song

OF THE WORLD

The Decoded Treasure of Nostradamus

Application of the keys of order to the quatrains of the famous *Centuries* revealed so vast a panorama of graphs and countergraphs based on the numbers of the quatrains that an ultimate cryptographic analysis of the words seemed improbable. The discovery, however, of the key to the rhymes, which showed how the quatrains—once put in their proper order—revealed a new metric sense different from the traditional one, made me suspect that other systems of encoding might also be present in this work.

The existence of parallel universes, from which all prophecy ensues, implies a temporal multiplicity other than the space and time we perceive. A multitemporal density exists of which we glimpse only fragments and traces in so-called three-dimensional reality. This density can be seen and known further than ever before, because modern humankind has at its disposal the extraordinary invention of the computer, which allows us a complexity and celerity of calculation all but unthinkable only a decade ago.

So when Gianni Posella from Rome told me that he had been working for years on a Nostradamic anagram based on the phrase contained in the stone of Turin, placed there by the prophet in 1556, I was not greatly surprised. The phrase obtained was the following:

ESAMINA PRESTO RIME CHIUSE NELL'ISOLA
   DRAGO
TU GIR PEL RIO E VIA COLLI
SEMINA LE MIE PERGAMENE

EXAMINE SOON THE RHYMES ENCLOSED IN
   DRAGON ISLAND
YOU WANDER BY THE RIVER AND THROUGH THE
   HILLS
SOW THE SEEDS OF MY PARCHMENTS

Mr. Posella did not understand the significance of this text, but I found in it a curious parallel with my own ongoing work. The "Dragon Island" situated in a river is the tiberine island in the Tiber River of Rome. As older Romans know, it came to be called Dragon Island because of the serpent of Aesculapius (*Dracon* in Greek) that adorned the prow of a stone ship erected a long time before to honor the god of medicine after he had brought an end to a plague epidemic in Rome. In modern times, I could well be the one wandering the fated hills seeking to disseminate his prophetic parchments!

Using the computer, I attempted to work out the procedure followed by Posella, which was based on the extraction of letters according to a sequence indicated by the date, 1556, carved above the engraved text. This particular method was extremely well known to Nostradamus's contemporaries, among whom were the Frenchman Blaise de Vigenère (1522–96) and the Italian mathematician and physicist Gerolamo Cardano (1501–76), the latter less noted for his studies of occult philosophy. These men, along with various other scholars, were intensely interested in systems of ciphering. By using grates or small perforated boxes, they were able to intercept letters hidden in the text according to a rhythmic key; naturally, in this day and age it makes more sense to use the computer. Mr. Posella, however, did not tell me how I would need to proceed once I had reached the end of the sculpted lines or where I must reposition myself to start over—he went away on vacation!

Luckily, software programs are extremely flexible and so one may proceed empirically, varying parameters and evaluating the results within a few seconds of attempts that by hand would have taken months. For the rest, I made use of the same technique by which, with the use of a computer, I had discovered the exact sequence of the quatrains. The letters discovered by Posella leapt out at me, revealing the precise means of the anagram he had studied.

During my varied experiments, I made another fortuitous discovery: By turning the ciphers of the date four times in one direction and then four times in the other (as there are four numbers in the date), Italian words appeared, forming the logical sentence *SENZA BISOGNO DI ALCUN ANAGRAMMA* (NEEDING NO ANAGRAM) with an occasional insertion of letters (inserted letters shown here below in lower case). One must begin with the "I" of the year "I556" and thus pass to the text—that is, "leap" the numbers and transform them into letters:

ITALIA HA SERVO ED E' A TO.qVi ONORE, AVGE MI VA. RESTA AI I.mi PASsi. Fa POI PATrian. QVI ONORE AvrA' E PROLE E' OnDA A vENIr. I FATI dEL TeMpo HA dA dIR

(ITALY HAS SERVED AND IS IV EN.hERe HONOR, TO MY REPUTATION. IT STAYS WITH My FOOTsteps. Makes THEN PATrian. HERE HONOR HE shall HaVE AND DESCENDENTS the WaVE TO cOMe. THE DESTINIES oF TiMe HE HAS TO teLL)

The stone of Turin, already known to many biographers, was photographed by Renucio Boscolo in 1975. Nostradamus refers to this in Quatrain 8 66. It is certainly not my intent to appropriate this discovery—all honors for it go to Boscolo—yet it is in this text (public property like the quatrains), that I discovered the formula for the stone's decryption, valid for both stone and quatrains, and which is my discovery alone.

In citing his descendants, Nostradamus again points out that our communal reality and memory may extend to times before the beginning of our physical and biological lives.

The matter of the stone of Nostradamus is also considered by Carlo Patrian in his book *Nostradamus—The Prophecies*.

Here is the inscription as it reads on the stone:

I556
NOSTRE DAMVS A LOGE ICI
ON ILIIA LE PARADIS LENFER
LE PVRGATOIRE IE MA PELLE
LA VICTOIRE QVI MHONORE
AVRALA GLOIRE QVI ME
MEPRISE OVRA LA
RVINE HNTIERE

Nostradamus has found lodging here where are Paradise, Hell, and Purgatory. I call myself Victory; who honors me shall have glory, who disdains me shall have complete ruin.

Nostradamus's inscription on the stone of Turin, deciphered according to the algorithm of the extraction of letters: four times 1-5-5-6 and four times 6-5-5-1- for 3 complete turns:

```
I(S S 6)
I     T     A     L     I         A   A'- S     ER    V    O  - E  - E'
-NOSTRE DAMVS A LOGE ICION IL IIA LE PARADIS LENFERLE PVRGATOIRE IE MA PEL
 5     5    61   5    5    61    5    5     61     5     5      6     6

    A   - TO:   qUi - On.- AU     G    E  - M    I  - V   A.R         E
  LELA VICTOIRE OVI MHONOREAVRALA GLOIRE QVI MEMEPRISE OVRA LARVINE HNTIERE
   5    51      6    5    51      6     5    51      6     5   51     5    5

     ST    A  - A     I   -     I.mi- PA    Ssi. Fà - P    O     I  - P
  NOSTRE DAMVS A LOGE ICION IL IIA LE PARADIS LENFERLE PVRGATOIRE IE MA PEL
   61    5    5   61    5    5    61    5     5      6      6      5   51

     A   T. - Qui - On.- Avr A' - E   -     PR    O    L     E  - E'
  LELA VICTOIRE OVI MHONOREAVRALA GLOIRE QVI MEMEPRISE OVRA LARVINE HNTIERE
   6    5    51      6    5    51      6    5    51      5     5   61     5

  On    DA - A'- vE    N    Ir.       I  - F       AT     I
  NOSTRE DAMVS A LOGE ICION IL IIA LE PARADIS LENFERLE PVRGATOIRE IE MA PEL
   5    61    5    5   61    5    5    6      6     5   51      6     5

  dEL - Te       Mpo- H A - dA - dIR.
  LELA VICTOIRE OVI MHONOREAVRALA GLOIRE QVI MEMEPRISE OVRA LARVINE HNTIERE
   51    6    5   51      6     5   51
```

The prophetic message hidden in the marble reveals Nostradamus's Italian interpreters to come in the twentieth century: R. Boscolo, C. Patrian, and finally, O. C. Ramotti, who will bear the name of Michele's son César. However, full decryption will be pursued only by the prophet's "offspring," that is, by those who adopt the method discovered by Cesare Ramotti. Interpreters who persist in focusing on the quatrains, which are actually a form of hermetic charade, without intuiting their development and solution through decryption into clearer statements, will gather only crumbs of the Nostradamic vision.

The result of what I call the "crumb-hunters'" interpretations is that they bring a lack of credibility to bear on the great seer himself. By such random interpretations of his prophecies they end in failure, which, curiously, never reflects on them but always on Nostradamus, who prophesied that they would bring him, for a time, to "complete ruin."

The inscription on the stone of Turin is, in fact, not an end in itself but the key of access to the clarification of all his predictions as well as those of his "offspring" in the future. Confirmation of this comes from the *Prophecies*.

In 1555 Nostradamus published his famous *Centuries* and *Prophecies*. It is interesting to note that these *Prophecies* are divided into 12 groups, each of which is headed by a specific year beginning with 1555. Yet prognostications do not refer to the years from 1555 through 1567, although the quatrains of the *Prophecies,* in every way identical to those of the *Centuries,* even indicate specific months in their headings. The prophet was laying down a false trail, hiding something else behind it.

To begin with, why would he have called them *Prophecies* if they were really identical to the *Centuries*? Because, in reality, they were none other than the *Century* beginning with 001, the first. Unwilling to call it *Century Zero,* he called it *Prophecies*.

By careful count, there should be 13 rather than 12 groups. By examining the dates attentively, however, we find that the group from the year 1556 is missing! This, of course, is the year he inscribed the stone of Turin. This indicates clearly that by inserting the stone's inscription in the group 1556, one should analogously be able to extend this method of decryption to the other quatrains.

Let us begin with 1555, Prophecy 1. Submitting it to a decryption identical to the one used on the stone of Turin, nothing significant happened. But the length and form of the two verses were not the same, so I thought to vary the key. It struck me that the date 1-5-5-5, being the year of publication of the whole work, was a more logical key than 1-5-5-6, which referred only to the inscription of the stone. With a few other very small modifications, the computer finally came up with the following phrase: *After the exact path, attentive rereading, by making mistakes you go deeper into the shadows, but you will learn.* [*In Italian: Dopo l'esatto sentiero rilettura attenta, fare erronea si va a peggiore tenebra, ma imparerai.*]

So now "the exact path," 1-5-5-5, the key to Nostradamus's whole gathering of future events, had been found, accompanied by a caveat: the decryptions must be read and reread attentively, since their meaning could not appear so clearly as that of the cited inscription.

Nostradamus, in fact, had composed a gigantic puzzle encompassing hundreds of texts. Indeed, it would seem that he must have had help from another dimension. This support is demonstrable in the decryption of *Prophecy 1,* in which the presence of divinity is affirmed.

Example of Decryption with the Key 1-5-5-5

As opposed to the stone, in the quatrains the words must be completed semantically and grammatically.

Quatrain 1 48 correlates with the illustration in Plate 66: the Sun and the Wheel of Nostradamus.

1 48

1 5   5 51 5 5   51 . . . etc.

When twenty years of the reign of the Moon have passed,
For seven thousand years another will hold the throne:
When the Sun takes up the days He left behind,
Then my prophecy is mined and done.

Vingt ans du regne de la Lune passez,
Sept.Mille ans autre tiendra sa monarchie:
Quand le Soleil prendra ses iours lassez,
Lors accomplit et mine ma prophetie.

In the first of the following lines are the letters extracted from the computer according to the sequence 1-5-5-5. In the second (intercalated with the third), the phrases are complete.

V d g n u a s s m a u t r a m c

Vedo già nelal Sua SS. Mano trama che

q i a u n e l n s s e i a n t i a o h

quel piau nella Luna fosse già anticipato poichè

u n n e a e s e p l n s r e sn i a

unione è Paese plus conoscere. Sogni da

g s r d e z t l s e n s a a e n t e

Gesù ridestata l'insensata gente,

d e L p z e a d a r d

dei lupi il peso se ne andare tardi.

d g e u a S m a u t r m c q a

Dirige una Somma autrice rime che qua da

u n l n s s e i a u t i a m o h u

una Luna venissero se chi aiutiamo hanno

l n e l a e s e p l n t r e o n i a e s r a e

Luna bella ed esemplare, plus intere regioni adesso superare

p t l s r e n s n a e n e

ponte illustre che ben sanare. Né

d L p z t e e d a a r d S

di là pesante viene danaro. Adesso

d g e L u a a M a t r r c Q o

dirigere Luna Matriarca qui ho

u n u n s s m i a u t i a m c h e l l e

una comunissima antica mia nautica macchina sulle

l n e s e i l n t i e o h i a e

lune. Sei lenti e cannocchiale. E ho chiave

e r a e e p l l s r e n s n i e n i

verace che plus lasciare. Nei sogni veni-

e d p z t l e e n d a a e d S l

re vedo pesanti leggende, onda avendo del Sole. Leg-

g e L p a e a d r r Q o

ge dei lupi là è a dare errore, quando

(o) p r s r s s o c c i m o i

presentirsi stesso Occidente morire. Ma morire

l l p r a s e r c o t m m a p e

quella paura se racconto Mamma pree e r e   i l z s o m i a h

vedere illusione solo mia che

i e n s o l a m p e n p e s

viene solare. Ma appena pesi

l n d e u a s L a p l t e   p r t

la Luna adegua, Sole apre plus te porta.

o   d r s r s s   o c l i   r o i

Può darsi russi occidentali trovi

l p r a s s   e r c i t m   m o   p e

l'opera adesso degli eserciti temo. Ma ove pe-

e r a i   e z s o t i a p h

netrarvi essoterica philosophia,

i e   s o l z m e n h e

cioè del Sole la semente, benchè

l n s e u a l a p e t e p e

quella inseguarla saprete, sempre

t d e   s r s   L o c l t r t i

tardare sarà. Se locali territori

p r s   s s o r c i   m m o i e

aprirsi, se esorcizzate memorie guer-

r a i e r s o   t m i   a p e / e

ra, diversi ho tempi sapere,

e i o l z s   m i n   h

se le violenze fossero minori. Che

n s   o u a   a p e n e p e

nostra Donna appena pene ne per-

d e u r s L a c l t e r t

de, versi solari ben diversi ascolterete.

Translation of the Decipherment of Quatrain 1 48

I see already in Her most sacred hand the web of the divine plan which in the Moon is already known and revealed so that the people might better know union.

The weight of the predator wolves will last until late, when the senseless people will be reawakened by Jesus from their illusions.

The Moon, greatest of authors, directs the rhymes of the prophecies that arrive here from Her. If those that we help have the beautiful and exemplary Moon, at this moment ever more regions are crossing the illumined bridge that heals.

Nor does heavy money come from there. In my present, here I am directing toward the Moons a very common ancient nautical machine.

Six lenses and and a telescope.

And I have a true key which is even more important to pass down. I see coming in my dreams heavy legends, receiving the wave of the Sun. The Law of the wolves is there to lay blame when it is foreseen that the whole Western world will die.

That fear must die if the tale of the Mother foretells more than my illusion that comes from the solar wave. But as soon as the Moon balances the weights, the Sun will open ever more His door.

I fear now lest this work be found by the armies of the Russians from the West. But wheresoever esoteric philosophy, which is the seed of the Sun, has penetrated, I shall know different times. Even if the sign of the opening of the door comes late, local territories will open. If the memories of war are exorcised and if violence is diminished. For as soon as you let go your sorrows, you will hear far different solar verses from our Lady.

The Roots of Nostradamus's Hermetic Tradition

The following comes from Nostradamus's letter to his son César, translated by Carlo Patrian:

> And although that occult philosophy (of prophecy) was not disapproved of, I have never wanted to share these inspired writings, although various volumes that had remained hidden for long centuries have been revealed to me. But being uncertain as to what might happen [if they were found], after I had read them I made a gift of them to Vulcan, and when he came to devour them the flame rose up to lick the air and produced an unusual and extremely clear light, clearer and brighter than natural flame, like the swift flash of lightning, which suddenly illuminated the house as if there

had sprung up in it a dazzling conflagration.

And so that they would not be abused in times to come by those seeking perfect transformation, whether lunar or solar, or searching for incorruptible metals in the bowels of the earth or the waves of the occult, I reduced them to ashes.

And so it would seem that the ancient secret of divination based on hermetic texts was destroyed. Though apparently not forever, given that Nostradamus adds later in his letter:

> But being seized by inspiration many times a week, and by lengthy calculations, I have gathered together some books of prophecy, each one containing one hundred astronomical and prophetic quatrains which I have attempted to compose in a somewhat abstruse manner: these are prophecies extending far into the future, from now until the year 3797.
>
> To see such a long period in time will no doubt baffle most people, yet beneath the concavity of the Moon it will have its place, and the causes of this knowledge will be universally understood throughout all the earth, my son.

All will one day be revealed, but until that day all must remain hidden. Are we now nearing the age of clarity when our houses will be illuminated by the light of the "dazzling conflagration" of multidimensional certainties? The translation of the prophecies arising from the eternal Intelligence is certainly underway. Thanks to indications left by the great prophet himself, the necessary calculations have been found, both in the texts of the *Centuries* and *Prophecies* and in the commemorative stone erected in Turin in Via Lessona in 1556, in which is encrypted the message that his interpreters in Italy will be three: Renucio Boscolo, Carlo Patrian, and his descendant—perhaps he who bears the name of the son to whom he dedicated his prophetic book.

But before the year 3797 many more interpreters will come, because that which Nostradamus bequeaths us is not a simple system for interpreting the quatrains, but a genuine cosmic and universal language by which we may connect with the "lunar intelligence."

The Secret of the Cabala

Nostradamus's father was a scholar of the ancient Cabala. His grandfather, Giovanni Nostradonna, a Jew from Sicily, came to St. Rémy in Provence following the troops of Carlo d'Angiò. It is probable that Nostradamus, although Catholic, inherited from his forebears an ancient knowledge along with the hermetic texts, as well as an intimate acquaintance with the Italian language, which he perfected both through contact with Italian sailors in Marseilles and during his travels in Italy.

It is said that Nostradamus visited the Sistine Chapel while Michelangelo worked there—and it is possible that he provided some inspiration for the artist's fantastic fresco of the Last Judgment. It seems Nostradamus also had some contact with Leonardo da Vinci. This contemporaneity of universal geniuses can be no accident. It came about at the first unfurling of the epoch of modern man, laboriously emerging from the darkness of the Middle Ages. During the Renaissance an occult literature flourished that derived from ancient hermetic texts dating back, according to tradition, to Melchisedek, the priest of God, eternally living, who initiated Abraham in the esoteric teachings that gave rise to the Cabala.

Raffaele Bessi says, in the August 1994 issue of *Giornale dei Misteri*:

> The Hebrew alphabet is the language God used for creation. Based on scripture, the Cabalist Abulafia developed a theory of mystical contemplation of these letters, given and understood as contributing parts of the Name of God, which contains in itself all of created reality, an absolute entity reflecting the secret sense and the totality of existence.
>
> The true ecstatic world is the world of letters and every letter of every language, springing from the original Hebrew tongue, can be used as a means of pursuing mystic ecstasy through the scientific study of their combinations.

Beginning with the articulation of possible permutations and combinations of letters, writing them and contemplating their written essence, one may proceed at last from writing to thought and from thought to the pure meditation of all these objects of "mystical logic": The articulation, the writing, and the thought from three overlapping levels of meditation.

THE TREE OF THE SEFIROT, USED FOR "HOKMÀT HATSERÙF," THE SCIENCE OF COMBINING LETTERS FOR A PROPHETIC READING OF THE BIBLE.

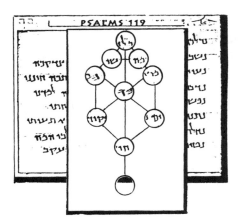

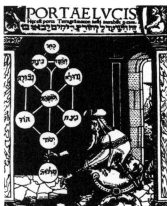

Comprehension of the one God is represented by a cognitive process unifying the intellect with the intelligible and the act of intellectualization. In actuality, the identification of the seeker with the object of his research corresponds to the union of the human intellect with the agent intelligence of the medieval Arabic-Judaic Aristotelian tradition.

After contemplation of the ten Sefirot, understood not so much as divine attributes but, rather, as revelatory indications of the agent Intelligence, the Cabalist can proceed to meditation on the twenty-two letters of the Hebrew alphabet, which represent a more profound level of understanding of the sacred text, the Torah, by way of the Path of Names.

Setting aside any conclusions on the ecstatic heights that were the purpose

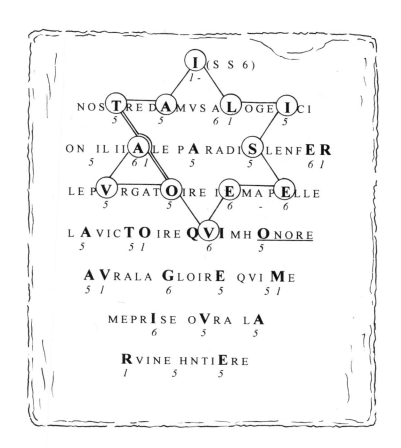

DECRYPTION OF THE STONE OF TURIN (FIRST TURN).

of the medieval Cabalists, it is natural to assume that the Tree of the Sefirot had a very ancient and more concrete origin and that only later, in the Middle Ages, did it give rise to mystical-philosophical-esoteric speculations. If not, what was this combinatory "science" of the letters based on?

The Tree of the Sefirot is represented by ten small circles connected by lines, resembling a hole-based coding system. A plate pierced just so, at regular intervals, could be placed upon the Torah, and the divine letters that appeared in the openings, when read in sequence, allowed the reader to travel the exact path—the true significance of the sacred words.

This particular system of ciphering has been used since the dawn of time and it is still used in modern times. In an old Clark Gable film we see a Russian spy place a handkerchief pierced with holes over a letter to read the hidden message.

The Cabalistic Nature of the Stone of Turin

In an attempt to reconstruct the ancient occult science burned by Nostradamus, I made public in the October 1993 issue of *Quaderno Nuovo (New Notebook)* the method I used to decipher the hidden message in the walled inscription on Via Lessona in Turin. This is the method by which I was able to travel the exact path of decipherment, according to what appears in Prophecy number 1 in clear Italian, and the method which I used to decipher all the quatrains. Nonetheless, I have chosen to give only one computerized example. Obviously the computer could not have been the method used in ancient times for decoding, in that, to use Nostradamus's occult euphemism, the computer still lay in the concavity of the Moon.

With the aid of the "Zephirot" the stone can be read in Italian by the following algoithm of the date 1-5-5-6 four times and 6-5-5-1 four times, for three turns. The blanks count as letters.

"Italia servo ed è a TO (Torino). Qui onore, ange mi va. Resta ai primi passi. Fà poi Patrian. Qui onone arrà e prole é onda a venir. I fati del tempo ha da dir."

A second message appears in the Seal of Solomon (the hexagram) by combining the same letters differently and reading them counterclockwise:

TAO Avo qui è esiliato (Ancestral TAO is exiled here).

The Quatrains as "Living Thoughts"

In 1959 Roger Frontenac, an ex-Naval official in charge of military codes and the author of *La Clef Sécrete de Nostradamus (The Secret Key of Nostradamus)*, discovered a Nostradamic phrase—enigmatic and hermetically enciphered—which I quote here: *Flamen fidele coegi id vulgo a kabbalo oplevi in viva acta tam latenter densa ex HDMP fata hac culta sunt ob gratiae fidos Nostradamus fas obturavit a saxo.*

The translation, according to Maurice Garcon of the French Academy, is as follows:

I have faithfully gathered the inspiration of that which is vulgarly called the Cabala, and I have disseminated it in living documents, but condensed in a secret form. The predictions for the weeks of years have been concealed by the acronym HDMP (a Cabalistic number)* for those who believe in God's grace. Nostradamus has hidden the divine law under a stone.

This discovery was examined by Carlo Patrian in his book *Nostradamus— The Prophecies,* in which he finds Frontenac's future dates unsatisfactory. The reason, as is demonstrated by attentive reading of Quatrain 600, is now quite clear: One need not pursue literally the apparent meanings of the quatrains, which are only the "corona" of living documents condensed according to a secret code, hidden in the stone and of Cabalistic inspiration. By following the 5 in the holes, these can be expanded on in full to synchronize with the times—this as well as the fact that the quatrains have their own key to order, which in itself, however, does not clarify their profound and hidden significance.

There is a certain law of words in subtle energetic fields that allows for the formation of true dynamic texts—living as our thoughts live in their verbal expression. Thus a synchronicity between the time of the decipherment and the time implicitly to come in the quatrain is established, which in turn permits a written clarification. The intuition of synchronicity between events was discovered by Carl Jung in 1951. He intuited that there exists a holographic temporal picture in which all comparable particulars are connected in the instant even if they belong to different times, without the necessity of a cause-and-effect connection (acausal connection).

My methodology not only permits us to discover the hidden meanings in the quatrains of Nostradamus, but also allows us to process new texts on computer and obtain from them interpretations of the invisible dimensions in which we are immersed.

Using this "lens of César"—in that it was to his son that Nostradamus left his secrets—it becomes possible to observe and even dialogue with the intelligent multidimensional universe of which we are part. Because it is from the other side of this same "lens" from which we are being communicated with, even if in code. We are dealing with an optic system that translates cosmic

---

*According to common numerology, based on the equivalency of letters to numbers, we have: H=8. D=4, M=13, P=16. Working the sum and then the numerological reduction, we obtain 41 and therefore 4+1=5.

multidimensional thought into common linear thought, and vice versa. As with Galileo's telescope, one end magnifies while the other miniaturizes; or rather, it gives in one direction a vision of many dimensions and in the other a vision that is solely three-dimensional. Although I use this example to explain myself, in truth, it is not a matter of observing objects in space, but of translating informational structures that include their own evolution in the passing of time. Such structures are perhaps analogous to the cellular genetic code DNA, which contains information about the individual not only at birth but during his or her future evolution.

In classical times we can look to the ideas of Plato, whose hypothesis is now revealed as ever more probable as an informational substratum of physical form. You may call such thinking science fiction, but there have been too many confirmations to continue denying the evidence. The hypothesis of blind causality is destined to founder. It will transform into possibility, then probability, and finally certainty. The *acausal connections* will ever more reveal themselves to be the effects of a *superior causality*.

Certainly the rigorous structures of computer programs have permitted me to transcend the illusion that we are separate from the superior world. These programs demonstrate our profound unity with multidimensional thought.

Grammatical and Semantic Interpretation

The general meaning of the hidden phrases in the series of letters obtained from the quatrains—which is done by extracting them on the computer according to the key sequence 1-5-5-5 (as explained in the section "The Decoded Treasure of Nostradamus")—emerges from the identification of the most significant words, words that have a semantic content. These may be found intuitively if these words are already completely or almost completely formed, or by using electronic vocabularies created purposely to search through groups of generic characters in such a way as to obtain words by which the meaning is completed.

To interpret a fragmentary text, such as an inscription corroded by time or a partially obliterated ancient manuscript, cryptography suggests tracking down the longest words first, those having the most number of characters reducible to a word, setting aside for the moment any search for grammatical connections or "empty" words. During this procedure it becomes possible to glimpse forms of association between highly probable words, such as common idiomatic or colloquial phrases and grammatical agreements of gender and number. Some words may appear full and clear; still, one must guard against false meanings, which by an analysis of semantic and grammatical agreements may be distinguished from real ones.

Naturally, the semantic bonds of any locution strengthen the cohesion of word fragments that compose it. By augmenting the number of individual characters through the examination of more words, the probability of association grows exponentially: while three letters could represent a thousand words, seventeen letters can belong to one or two locutions at the most.

For instance, the saying *la fortuna aiuta gli audaci* (Fate helps the brave or God helps those who help themselves) is easily intelligible even when reduced to "l ftuna auta gl adaci," (fte hlps th brve), although taken by itself the phoneme "adaci" might also mean "predaci" (predators), clearly nonsense in the context. In this way one arrives at a comprehension of the general significance despite the fact that there is not yet a clearly structured discourse.

Obviously, if the text in question deals with religious or spiritual matters, the emergence of terms adapted to the description of natural catastrophes or medical science, to use two examples, can be discounted because they are not germane to the issue.

In this regard, the original French quatrain, understandable enough grammatically despite certain distortions, should always be the guide. Even the quatrain's more evident meaning will be enriched by the cryptographic revelation of its hidden message. By functioning as a sort of title or summary, it contributes to the clarity of the whole. According to Nostradamus a day will come when the prophecies of the quatrains *seront plus esclarci* (will be clearer). I believe this day has come.

At any rate, the prophet added that he probably deserved some sort of punishment for having written verses that were at once so easy to grasp and so completely unintelligible. He meant by this that the quatrains would not, without their implicit explanations, be fully comprehensible to the reader.

Nostradamus frequently used an archaic Italian, heavily Latinate, semantic construction. Those who have studied Latin will have no difficulty with a direct reading of the interpretation obtained from the computer (in full under the line of letters). It is like trying to translate Cicero or Caesar into Italian or English: to track down the subject you have to hunt through the whole phrase, and very often the last word in the sentence turns out to be the crucial verb.

In order to render them more understandable to humanity today, I am constantly working to paraphrase these texts. This involves no more than a reshaping of each sentence into the prosaic and arid constructions of modern language, although this renders them more banal, divesting them of the poetic dimension inherent in ancient writings.

At times the completion of these transcendental puzzles has required the use of French terms, usually in the "empty" words of grammatical connectors. Thus you may see, albeit rarely, *tous, vous, que, ville,* and so on, as well as abbreviations such as "i.e." and "Phi" for "philosophy."

Once the salient reference points in a word are fixed, one can fill in the gaps in accordance with the original semantic hypothesis, respecting both grammar and spelling. One must remember, however, that in ancient usage the *v* and *u* were interchangeable and the *f* was read as an *s*; there are also a few other necessary orthographic adjustments.

Little by little the entire puzzle is completed and even the empty words find their proper place. But sometimes the complete constructed sentence makes no sense in light of logic and grammar, at which point the operative hypothesis must be discarded in favor of alternative words. Although this procedure may need to be repeated a number of times, in the end I have always been rewarded by a clear and complete meaning. This is the binding rule: The sentence must make sense—because the *exact path* of decipherment exists in every case and was prophesied in the cryptographic message of Prophecy number 1.

The predicted events have occurred, are occurring, or will occur, and thus the whole system functions more or less pragmatically. Naturally there are some possible variants, but I have noticed that these exert a very slight influence on the general significance of the interpretation. By whatever unknown means it happens, both variants result in sentences that confirm rather than oppose each other.

This is not to say that I can offer up absolute certainties, but a significant percentage are valid. Out of ten predictions, about eight are verifiable. At one time I devoted myself to an analogous work in order to demonstrate the possibility of a computer arriving at an "intelligent" reading of a text. Starting with an automatic grammatical analysis, I came up with a demonstration program in which the computer managed, on its own, to distinguish parts of speech in a given text without the help of dictionaries.

In good time I shall resume this subject and apply it to the work in question. There is much on the semantic and grammatical level that even a computer can discover. This could be a stimulating field of research for young (and not-so-young) computer programmers of the future.

Technical Limits of Reading Hidden Text

Because processing the quatrains can be accomplished in a completely technical way, we may suppose that their implicit content does not spring from any sort of extrasensory origin, but instead is a matter of normal mental calculations. These calculations may derive from the subconscious without being transcendental precognitions.

However, the hidden Italian writing contained in the stone of Turin—writing based on a very ancient tradition of clear Cabalistic imprint, demonstrates an evident prophetic knowledge of the Italian interpreters of the future. I can demonstrate that many of the predictions obtained by a cryptographic reading have already been fulfilled, while others are statistically probable future events. Up to what point, then, can we obtain a valid response?

If any combination at all of phonemes can be introduced into the processing mechanism of a computer, according to the Cabalistic key of Nostradamus first and the mental key afterward, perhaps we may always expect a morphologically and semantically acceptable answer. This would be improbable, in that semantically deficient, with a random combination of characters; in other words, you can't get blood out of a stone. But I think that even disconnected texts, provided they have a sufficient morphological structure, may offer up some kind of answer, even where logic is lacking in the matrix text.

To me the validity of the Nostradamic-wave is undoubtable, as I have had so many demonstrations of connection with the quatrains; nonetheless, hypothetically it is possible that there are other methods as yet unknown. I imagine an interchange of universal information with Jungian-type archetypes, intelligent, collective, and impersonal.

A computer program is perfectly intelligent. It is not true that it is mindless; it could not function in any way with less-than-perfect intelligence, although, in technical terms this intellectual content derived from humanity is called only skill or ability. At the same time it is totally impersonal and devoid even of conscience. The world-class chess champion Kasparov was defeated by a subhuman electronic program that is for sale everywhere.

Any electroencephalogram will reveal the presence of various kinds of brain waves. It is not farfetched then to hypothesize the existence of mental and verbal waves as well. Already experiments are underway using these waves to affect and direct the computer.

This universal archetype of the Nostradamic-wave can be used literally to obtain atemporal knowledge about individual persons. In the mental and verbal waves implicitly present in a single individual's writing, one may discover echoes of the Nostradamic-wave by processing the writing on the computer according to the method previously described.

It is my hypothesis that in an oracular request regarding one's own destiny, the Nostradamic-wave merges with that of the interrogant and interacts, not instantaneously, but atemporally with the formulation of the phrases, which will therefore implicitly contain the response already in verbal language. If I am the interrogant, the answer will be in Italian. According to the Cabalists, all languages are valid because they all derive from the original sacred language: in the beginning there was the Word, and the Word was with God.

There has been a long controversy between psychology and spiritualism as to whether so-called paranormal phenomena are psychological by nature or attributable to external entities that possess a separate existence. This is reminiscent of an analogous dispute that took place in the world of physics, concerning whether light was made up of particles or waves. The conclusion, of course, was that both aspects were realistically valid and demonstrable and only seemingly in apparent contradiction to each other. The same may be true of extrasensory phenomena: the psychological and spiritual manifestations are interconnected.

One guide/entity (Beverini, GdM 275) expresses it like this: "If there were, on the part of the human creature, the liberty to act in full conscious-ness, that creature would become consciousness itself, and therefore truth."

If I assume the consciousness of being César, Nostradamus's son, or even Nostradamus himself, this is not in any physical or reincarnative sense. It is this simple: whoever desires to *be* him must enter into his logical archetype while reading the ciphered texts obtained from the computer and resonate within this text *as if* in a dialogue with him. When Nostradamus wrote that his "descendants" would tell the fates of the times, he may have been refer-ring to the "César" who is now objectively trying to do so, but in reality he is also addressing a whole series of incarnate descendants who may also tell, thanks to this method, the fates of the times. Quite probably his predecessors did the same, going back as far as Hermes Trismegistus, without, however, any need of the computer!

So-called esoteric manifestations, which are found in the traditions of all epochs, must not therefore be despised but attentively followed and studied. Today this is true more than ever in that the computer offers us the physical capacity for extremely swift calculation.

KEY TEXT: BRANCH IV/MILLENNIUM, 10 QUATRAIN 7 05

The wine will be spilled on the table,
The Third will not have what it wants,
But from Parma a second black one is sent
Who will work his will from Perugia to Pisa.

PLATE 55: CRUET AND SCEPTER WITH THREE POINTS LIKE A LILY.

Sarà il vino sulla tavola versato
Il Terzo non avrà quel che pretende
Di Parma un secondo nero mandato,
Da Perugia a Pisa farà quello che intende.

Vin sur la table en sera respandu
Le tiers n'aura celle qu'il pretendoit,
Deux fois du noir de Parme descendu,
Perouse a Pize fera ce qu'il cuidoit.

The ecclesiastic rites of the church will be changed. Although the Third Reich will be defeated, a new strongman will rise up in Italy—the romagnolo Mussolini.

Decryption

The divine Wine of every day is lost.

The ritual significance of Holy Communion is lost, and the Church withdraws its support from a strong-arm government. Discord erupts among the clergy when the pope who uses an airplane can no longer travel due to contrary winds.

The Franciscan priests will leave the Church.

Demagogic oratory takes over television. Humankind will free itself from religious, but not from political, fanaticism. "Faith will offer the cures and evil will be forgiven," but even if we are liberated from fatal heresies, they "weave black sacks for you."

Division erupts when, because of a question posed by a "German Jesuit," the pope is disturbed by "the heresies of the demon, who slips into our customs under his rude black flag hoping there is some treasure to be salvaged."

Here is a parallel with the past that explains the figure in the following plate: a serpent sowing precious seeds, next to a chalice adorned with a lily, the emblem of the Medici.

*I saw the sorrows caused by the serpents. Yesterday I saw them give a squalid
rosary of gold to a harsh and rigid master. He has his own men with him even
in the city of Rome. Because the Pontiff prefers usefulness to patronage, this
descendant will follow him well and he will cease to be a master.*

A concept understood in the time of Paul III Farnese, Paul IV Carafa, and
Pius IV de Medici, the nepotistic and intransigent popes of the Council of
Trent in the epoch of Nostradamus, was that of a Prince of the Church who
protected the arts so that artistic masterpieces would bring prestige to the
Church itself. Yet greater good will come when the concept of private own-
ership of earthly possessions by the religious institutions collapses completely.

*Those ten days were hard ones. When you would hear the Father, voices and music
resounding. You will have a peaceful pontiff who gives thought to the piteous
sorrows of the living and honors their trials, giving out roses. The lights of this orator are being lit now in his immense Office.*

The new orator, who will make manifest the voice of the Father to the
faithful, will be surrounded by the light of communion with the universal
conscience.

Three almost annihilated by the Antichrist.

Twenty-seven years of blood shall his war last.

The heretics dead, captive, exiled,

The rivers red with blood and human bodies, hail on earth.

Dall'Anticristo tre ben tosto annichiliti

Venti e sette anni di sangue durerà sua guerra

Gli eretici morti, prigionieri, esiliati,

Di sangue e corpi umani i corsi arrossati, grandine in terra.

L'Antechrist trois bien tost annichilez.

Vingt et sept ans durera sa guerre.

Les heretiques morts, captifs exilez.

Sang corps humain eau rogie gresler terre.

PLATE 58: GRYPHON OR DRAGON WITH THE POPE'S SHEPHERD CROOK. (SEE COLOR PLATE 58.)

Decryption

The last years do not make happy reading. They understand nothing about the tragedies of history as long as the ancient instincts continue. There is great crisis, evil years. Even if the waiting is tiring, you shall feel a rebirth of that goodness by which you will heal.

Those who live will feel the burden of the arrogant, angry counsels of power rejecting the exotic, drowsy peoples of the Dragon who admire intemperate women.

There will come a cure for these troubles when the waters cease, and the age shall be renewed as long as they come to a halt and return immediately to follow more gladsome paths. Here would be the joyful priests, all gladly dressed in linens of the angels, joining with the women, and it is when they join with the women that I feel the wheel of Selene coming to its end.

What shadows will fall on the surrendered British lands, much more if the Russians are the same sad assassins.

In the East, disloyal Chinese scientists will persist; they will confiscate the merchandise. They have a general who may provoke a cruel onslaught. War breaks out, and a group comes swiftly to the fore, to attack. In the East the sad sciences unleash a great power. Fear the Chinese physicist, as they are in terrible confusion. In the Orient they are working to make war break out again, the promoted path is a great mistake. The tempest comes down, great massacres occur. These same murderers in the East risk great crises, in which they implement purges that reach even those in asylum.

From Selene I have rumors of a great horror, a presentiment of future aggression.

March 20, 1995: aggressive chemicals are dispersed throughout the city of Tokyo by a fanatic organization. Hideo Murai, a Japanese physicist suspected of fabricating the nerve gas, is murdered on television on April 23, 1995. The event echoes the case of Lee Harvey Oswald who was also very dramatically eliminated—for having killed Kennedy? Or to cover up other secrets?

KEY TEXT: BRANCH V/MILLENNIUM, 6 QUATRAIN 2 50

When those from the lands of Europe
See England set up her throne behind
Her flanks, there will be cruel wars.
The ancient plague will be worse than enemies.

Quando quelli, d'Europa dalle terre
Vedranno l'Inghilterra prima che sia messo il seggio
Dietro le spalle, quando saran crudeli guerre
La vecchia piaga, del nemico sarà peggio.

Quand ceux d'Hainault, de Gand et de Bruexelles
Verront a Langres le siege devant mis,
Derrier leurs flanc seront guerres cruelles.
La plaie antique sera pis qu'ennemis.

Decryption

The throne of the reign of peace will come, but before its advent the partners of Europe will see England tormented by an ancient plague: the Irish revolt in Ulster incited by Catholics and Protestants. After twenty-five years the IRA will approach the government in London, but the English subjects of Belfast, fearing a plot to abandon them, will continue the struggle. Another plague will wreak more havoc than war in Russia.

Radioactive pollution from nuclear sites. The danger represented by Chernobyl is not forgotten.

Those folk drink quantities of brandy, but it kills them. They experience an unnatural ecstasy through the tankards and tumblers of the tavern, and because their cold, weak earth cannot sustain garlic and vegetables, they grow oats and adulterate them infernally, bringing home to others the error of slavery to drink. These are an honorable people, but they are suicides; they will drink so much they become idiot dissidents. They will dishonor ethnic groups and invade two seats of government where the great Anglican walls will be closed against them, exacerbating the followers of the IRA. The beseiged citizens will cry out in vain and lapse back into the alluring idea of reinstating British rule, so that seeing this reaction, the aggregate will dissolve. The stepsister will come to remove the aggressors themselves, if with shouting and confusion the City retaliates for the acts of criminal, irresponsible men who are draining the money.

The city of London, a temple to business, is tired of Irish dissidence, which is draining the finances. It would like to come to an agreement even at the risk of setting off a counterreaction on the part of the Protestant citizens of Ulster.

When the zealous Slav came at great risk to restructure the Russian lands, when a new quarrel of black shouting erupted, it set off madness, black dangers; even the bisextile six leads to misery on the paved earth of the republic.

Incredible as the use of a carcinogenic irritant may be, if they do not do something more about the emission, when the mixture of black air rises, it will be deadly. A three-pointed star will make you inhale the airs of the sky and cut down the city. And they will be afraid that now, along with the demolition of their houses with excavators, the people are being poisoned at "six" by the waters of insane energies, when synchonistically the star reveals to us how badly polluted they are.

Even if these peoples reach peace, they will suffer the after effects of old troubles. Fatally, they will insist on using sources of the most serious kind of pollution. The polluted zones will be marked by a three-pointed star indicating contamination by radiation or poisonous substances.

"Three kings" have afflicted humanity throughout the entire hundred-year span of the twentieth century. Possessed of very different ideologies, yet similar in the totalitarian and demanding spirits that characterized them, they have perpetuated an age-old evil. These three kings are also mentioned in Quatrain 28 of Branch XXIII (1 81) by the Greek initials Kappa, Theta, and Lambda.

This is confirmed by the three alphabetic figures shown. The first is a

PLATE 60: THREE ARCHAIC LETTERS: LAMBDA, THETA, KAPPA. THE OVERTURNED CHALICE SPROUTS A FLOWER. EAGLE WITH OLIVE BRANCH.

Phoenician/Semitic *Lamedh* from which the Greek *Lambda* derives (rotated 180 degrees and preceding the Latin letter *L*). The second is a Phoenician/Semitic *Tau* derived from the Egyptian cross. The helmet of the Prussian Kaiser represents the *Kaph* of the Phoenician alphabet. In Latin it becomes *C*, but *Caesar* was pronounced *Kesar* from which came *Kaiser*, who at the beginning of the century was Emperor Wilhelm II.

Ka has another esoteric meaning having to do with the corporal spirit cited in the quatrain, a spirit dominating the world in place of the true divine spirit. For the Egyptians, *Ka* was one of the elements from which man was formed, *genius* or *vital power* or even *the etheric double or the possibility of adoration of the divine*, which permitted him to live on in the afterlife. The *Ka* together with the *Ba* (soul) and the *Akh* (spirit) form the archetype of the Hebrew *Ka-ba-laq*, which after the Exodus from Egypt represented the esoteric substance of the divine language hidden in the infinite night of time.

Hermetic philosophy teaches that the *Ka* can become assimilated by the vital body, which is opposite in sex to the physical body. This probably corresponds to the animus and anima put forth by Jung. In her book *Intuitive Science*, physicist Giuliana Conforto maintains that the individual vital body is a vortex of the collective vital sea, which appears to the eye of the clairvoyant as a most luminous Sun—not the sun visible to the physical eye, but the true and only source of Life. This is the great Central Sun, the Cosmic Sun from which we all spring like rays from a star. These concepts of the "universal sea" and the "central sun" are also present in the encoded writings of Nostradamus.

When the earthly aspect of the individual *Ka* gains the upper hand in humankind, it manifests as a detachment from the universal Spirit. The Holy See manifests this same alienation from Spirit, thus abetting society's decline into corruption and greed for power and material wealth.

In this decadent era appear the three kings: the Kaisers, the Tyrants, and the Lunars (or followers of the Crescent Moon). Imperial aristocracy is put to an end in 1918 after a terrible worldwide conflict. The autocracies of the dictators (the three brothers who placed the world in torment—Stalin, Mussolini, and Hitler) endure until after the second world war. The wave of anti-West sentiment set into motion by the followers of Ayatollah Khomeini, Muamar Gheddafi, and Saddam Hussein will not subside until the very end of the millennium.

The Holy See no longer rules secularly or temporally but by maintaining the structure of an absolute monarchy—even with so little territory—and by extending it throughout the planet, this absolute monarchy perpetuates the defects of an antidemocratic authoritarianism, which is by this time entirely obsolete. Whether in the East or in the West, true faith is not based on absolutes or fundamentalisms, but on ethical self-awareness. Both socially and spiritually humanity must grow individual by individual.

KEY TEXT: BRANCH IV/MILLENNIUM, 2 QUATRAIN 8 99

By the power of three kings of the world
The Holy See shall be moved to another place
Where the substance of the corporal spirit
Will be received and welcomed as true faith.

Per la potenza di tre Re nel temporale
In altro luogo messa Santa Sede:
Ove sostanza di spirito corporale
Sarà rimessa e accolta come vera fede.

Par la puissance des trois Rois temporels,
En autre lieu sera mis le sainct Siege,
Ou la substance de l'esprit corporel
Sera remis et receu pour vrai siege.

Decryption

The sects of the three kings will have passed in seven thirty-three. You shall see houses made whole again, Europe relieved of the pain of her sorrows, an evil millennium, in which exile weighed me down.

By this time, the "three kings" belong to the past; Quatrain 7 33 refers explicitly to the tyrant, Hitler. The spirit of Nostradamus was "in exile" in the sixteenth century.

I await that season in which they join together in useful and joyful marriages. I feel the seductive reptile instigating the heretic peoples of Russia, that only yes-

terday reddened history with blood. A queen returns, crowned mistress of the land of windmills.

In the time of the kaisers and czars, Russia caused the first world war and will provoke yet other crises. Now Free Europe has taken over from the emperors and organized the European Economic Community (EEC). Agreements of Maastricht in Holland in 1993.

Wherever hatreds flame the fan of evil, there shall emerge that heavy, serious, and insensate epidemic of the bestial red star of yesterday's Soviet Russia, trying to return to the murderous era of terror. All my visions of them lead equally to the way of evil. From the United States to the Soviet Union, inspections reveal heavy threats. Now the ultimate crises strangle all.

New conflicts arise between the United States and Russia, since Zirinowsky attempts a return to the epoch of the Nazi tyrants, stirring up an exacerbated nationalism.

The Libyan sky will burn before long. Then the time of their shouting is done. Israel is seen to become a land of the poor. Saddam would have you marry the Koran, which contains a treasure. And my Centuries shall well please eternal Rome and also the Heavens, if the gold I have hidden turns out to be real and pure, the echo of the passing of ages.

The "Lambda kings" are the Islamic followers of the flag of the Crescent Moon. Despite new clashes with the fundamentalists, Gheddafi is no longer bombarded. The Middle East evolves. Israel welcomes the Palestinians. Saddam accumulates treasures with his hydrocarbons. According to the auspices of Nostradamus's *Centuries,* even in Rome, the flowers of a new era shall bloom from the overturned chalice, if the passing of time has not clouded their echo.

The stories will be exposed once again now, even if they are but accorded mention; for this reason I shall try to split into twinship two remote times, for there will be more editors there [in the future] *to disseminate these revelations. I shall dare to receive the echo-wave originating from the sacred transmitters.*

Historical events are displayed by means of an echo-wave that can be revealed and demonstrated by modern computerized decryptions.

KEY TEXT: BRANCH X, 26 QUATRAIN 1 00

Longtime a gray bird will be seen in the sky
In France as in the Tuscan land:
When it holds in its beak a young green branch,
Then a great one will die and the war will end.

Per tanto in cielo sarà visto grigio uccello
Così in Francia come in Toscana terra:
Poi nel becco recando un verde ramoscello,
Allor morirà un grande e finirà la guerra.

Longtemps au ciel sera veu gris oiseau,
Aupres de Dole et de Toscane terre,
Tenant au bec un verdoiant rameau,
Mourra tost grand et finira la guerre.

Foreseen here in Nostradamus's encoded and decrypted message is publication of the new interpretations of the *Centuries* based on a mathematical analysis by the computer and taken with the original autographs and illustrations. The quatrain refers to the end of World War II. After the death of a great one—President Franklin Roosevelt—peace would be brought to the world by the American Eagle. Since that time there have been no more global wars. Now it is up to us to live in such a way that we will never see a world war again.

KEY TEXT: BRANCH XXIII, 28 QUATRAIN 1 81

From the new human herd shall be set apart
From judgement and counsel detached,
Their strongholds divided in many parts,
Kappa, Theta, Lambda: dead, banished, cut off.

Da masse umane nuove saran messi da parte,
Da giurisdizione e governo distaccati,
Lor piazzaforti divise in più parti,
Kappa, Theta, Lambda, morti, banditi, stroncati.

D'humain troupeau neuf seront mis à part,
De iugement et conseil separez,
Leur fort divisé en depart,
Kapg, Thita, Lambda mors bannis esgarez.

Decryption

More geological material dust from the meteors will come if the arcane UFOs fly through and beyond the solar system. Those who envision following them are mad. Eurovision will make use of a hermetic seal if they become aware of an unexpected tactic on the part of the United States. It is thought that they come to generate troubles and corrode our principal faiths, that by collapsing the Middle European dam they will corrupt solidarity in every country. But if they come into Eurovision they will implement good, sane sacraments without meaningless rites—they are not abstract executioners.

These etheric beings will return us to our original faith, overturning the alien, dogmatic, gothic, and decadent obstacles placed before the student of Palaeochristianity. The dawn resumes, leading Europe to the finish. I tell you that the UFOs will come in honesty, and if their advent leads to heuristic conflicts, the United States will be responsible for a union of faith that deludes the people less.

The civilization of madness falls quiet. The pious mother will leave the cities

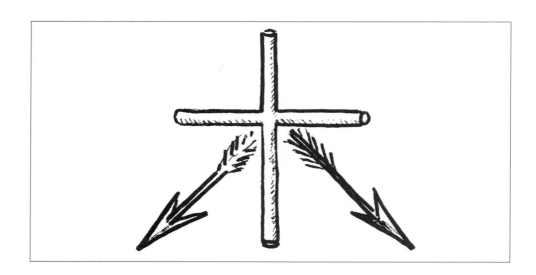

PLATE 61: CROSS AND THUNDERBOLTS.

of sloth, and it will fall to the father—the pope—to render them whole once again. The magistrates shall be abased, and my good people will come to be blessed. They will abandon the sciences, if the epoch of the city of asses arises, amply deceived by the paid ambassador of an immoral king. An edict forbids abortion except in dire necessity, since it betrays the sensibility of the sex. In the oasis scant punishment touches the abusers, though I fear many will fail; once the good folk are embarked and on board, snow will fall on the unconscious masters.

Here is a preview of the life of the papal encyclical *Evangelium Vitae* of March, 1995. Science must not agitate against ethics. The law on indiscriminate abortion will be revised with a decree. Oblivion, not punishment, will be the lot of men without judgment.

KEY TEXT: BRANCH VI/MILLENNIUM, 15 QUATRAIN 1 91

The gods will appear to humankind,
The future authors of great conflict,
Before the sky clears, lances and swords:
The left shall suffer great affliction.

Gli dei faranno agli umani apparizione
Agli autori che saran del gran conflitto
Prima che il cielo sia sereno, spade e lance:
Ché a sinistra sarà grande afflizione.

Les dieux feront aus humains apparence,
Ce qui'ils seront auteurs de grand conflict,
Avant Ciel veu serain espee et lance,
Que vers main gauche sera plus grand afflict.

Decryption

In the country of the lira, Marseillese-type reprisals instigate delusional exercises in the art of shutting down. The rumor of crisis always leads to an increase in the number of believers, even if that faith is pernicious, as in the case of the followers of Fascism.

Forza Italia (Italian Force) will suffer reprisals of a *Marseilles-type* (populist rising against the established powers): the battalions of the revolutionary hymn against the decrees of Berlusconi will go on the march. The great demonstrations of the unions in Rome on December 11, 1994—which caused a significant shift on the part of the voters toward more moderate parties—were already over. The extreme right was still judged to be dangerous.

They have true peace here, who use the law well. But as you know, one finds hierarchies in gold, and more will come to augment the rumors of killings, crises, and conflicts.

Only if they understand how to use the Christian laws well will there be peace between these political parties. As in the years of lead (1970–1980, a decade of terrorism and the Red Brigade), social struggle based on the fundamental imbalance between classes will cause deadly conflicts. Even the Vatican hierarchy will become involved.

The Centuries overflow with human passions, and for years I thought of one of my most honest students writing them down—these details of an epoch it is hard to admire, not knowing by what other causes these followers will win through and emerge from the ruinous clash reconciled.

Contrary to what some believe, the prophetic verses are not to blame for the disasters they prophesy, but unfortunately they are themselves a mirror of the ignorant masses who are unaware of causes, the knowledge of which elevates humanity to service to the divine plan that will ultimately prevail no matter what we think or do.

If they intend to devour the West, our Pentecost appears to be far distant. Where fatal quarrels occur, overriding the peace that Heaven grants to Europe, you will see the rebirth of the waters' rage and witness fire on the Tiber. Some will manage to win an uncertain referendum: if it comes to fruition, the churches which are even now failing will fall quiet at seven.

After mortal conflicts have consumed the West, the Pentecost—that is, the descent of the Spirit—now far in the future, will restore peace, probably in 1998. At that time the angelic beings will reveal themselves to us, manifesting quite clearly in what we now consider to be evanescent extraterrestrial phenomena. But in 1997 the churches, not only those linked to religion, but also political parties, will fall silent. In 1996 we may see the Tiber in flood. An uncertain electorate in Italy will result in a government that reduces the failed "churches" to silence.

An important grandson will emerge from Italy. Those who heal with humanity and serve it will be fulfilled and render aid to the city since the clerics of the Tiber will have been shut up harshly in austere cells where they will be kept without license to even emerge to light incense in the churches, if the law of egalitarianism comes to be practiced.

Those who govern Rome in the name of equality, other than by filling prison cells with clerics impartially condemned, must heal the city with humanity.

Due to inertia, humanity will face the great problem of division; the waters shall be driven to roil, and in the Quirinal they will celebrate a duke, showing a strong interest in the new enterprises he favors, approving his spectacular aspect and letting him sweep them up until a yet greater division occurs, men fighting like beasts.

Since a fatal inertia informing the work of restoration and healing will cause yet other divisions, the people will approve a new duke who proposes new and spectacular enterprises. But he will in fact only increase the divisions. At last the Pentecost, the descent of Spirit, will bring on a millennium of peace. In the decryption of Nostradamus's Sestet 11 57, published in the *Notebooks* July, 1993, this political prediction regarding events in Italy appears very clearly: "The Democratic proletarians will unite with the Populists, after which will come a persecution. You will see then how troops of soldiers can strip and loot the House." At the time of publication in 1993, there was not yet a glimpse of this political alliance, pregnant with consequence—the shift of the Christian Democrats to the far left. Possible future developments are pictured in Plate 79.

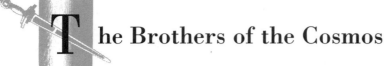

The Brothers of the Cosmos

KEY TEXT: BRANCH V/MILLENNIUM, 12 QUATRAIN 6 07

From the North to the Blacks, from Dace to Britain
To the United States, the Brothers will be oppressed,
Even by the Roman chief of Gallic blood,
And their copies will be hunted down in the forests.

Dal Nord ai Neri, dalla Dacia alla Britannia
Dagli Uniti i Fratelli son vessati
Dal capo Roman uscito da sangue Gallico,
E le lor copie per i boschi inseguite.

Norneigre et Dace, et l'isle Britannique,
Par les unis freres seront vexes,
Le chef Romain issu de sang Gallique
Et les copies aus forests repoulsees.

UFO phenomena are appearing in all parts of the world, testimony to a multi-dimensional intelligence, as well as to the existence of extraterrestrials. Far from being well received, these extraterrestrials will be actively hunted by British and American aviators. Androids sent out for the purpose of exploration will be set upon and captured in the woods, as in the case of Arquata of Tronto in October 1993. The quatrain published by the weekly magazine *Visto* may refer to that precise event. I had extracted the encoded comment in January of the same year, ten months before the events took place.

Even the pope—the Roman not of Italian blood—clearly stands against accepting beings from other planets as messengers of divine consciousness. This temporal reference synchronizes with the present, as well as with the end of the millennium.

I consider all I decipher as a scenario of possible and probable events affecting humanity today, not necessarily as what will actually occur. It is our collective will that decides the course of events, whether that course appears good or evil. We must ask only for greater awareness from our Higher Power, and for global understanding with which to determine our future.

It is heartrending to witness the age-old censure with which we treat—

and will continue to treat—other humans born in the infinite cosmos. Children of God, as are we, they try heroically to pull us out from under the shadow of predjudice and suspicion, to which our governments are totally dedicated. The path of evolution that will take us to the stars has long to go, but it is important that we begin to walk it now.

Excellent aliens, almost like heroes, from the joint stars of Leo and Taurus intend to unite the souls of believers, if they suffer confusion.

The provenance and purpose of the extraterrestrials are clearly described here: beings from the united zodiacal constellations of Leo and Taurus (therefore probably belonging to a galactic confederation) are coming to us soon to help the humans of planet Earth achieve the evolution that will unite the material world with the Spirit.

Decryption

Even as they proscribed the ecstasy of creation to humanity in the East, thus rendering it imbecile, revelation of the magic of the intellect threw the churches in Europe into confusion and turmoil. It were as if the same incarnated ones must once again eliminate the weight of the believers' heresies. But in my old exile, which I passed there, these esoteric quatrains were revealed to me from my own glad stars. If they unite with each other, my sisters shall have these words.

In atheistic Russia, spiritual thinking is derided and even in Europe the churches, as in the past, oppose every avenue of direct individual consciousness of the divine dimension. Here Nostradamus is confiding in us that in what he considered the "exile" of incarnation, his esoteric quatrains reached him directly from the stars. Today it is women—who he calls "sisters"—that have a clear perception of multidimensional mental messages and can most easily receive revelation, if only they unite and refuse to be divided by the dictates of lower interests.

I have seen the Chrononauts of goodwill waiting on the Moon to free the Churches from the danger that the arrival of the people of Sirius might occasion.

Originating from another planet, the Chrononauts are beings who can travel through time. An image of them received by a medium reveals them as beings with triangular faces and four-fingered hands. Human in form, but with major differences, they may disturb the human ideal we have of angelic entities.

The screens of the English have not allowed the extraterrestrials a peaceful descent. I have seen how many wise ones have been killed. The United States has been made to think that the angels are beasts, some kind of telepathic Russian animal. And all the English think of is hunting them down. And they themselves come down here and are killed by a defective kind of contact. It is imperative that Europe and the United States observe with respect the gifts from the stars, since it is rarest in those countries to find peers who will testify as to their thought.

The radar screens of the NATO powers intercept every UFO they find that is of a material nature. However, these beings are unable to assume an incarnate aspect. Many trial descents have failed due to hostile nations, fearful of losing their terrestrial power. There are, or will be in the future, attempts at contact in space that will fail. Hunting down and persecuting intelligent beings more evolved than ourselves is not a great demonstration of intelligence on our part.

Already they have hidden this so-called poem where there was a sentinel in the wintry time.

Perhaps knowing that we have always been helped by these superior brothers will at last shed a light of comprehension in the xenophobic atmosphere of hostility pervading our Earth—or as Dante wrote, "The flower bed that makes us so ferocious." A model of thought that knows no planetary confines must at last emerge victorious. And as with Dante, so another of their sentinels in the night of time was close to Michele Nostradamus, the Provençal brother.

KEY TEXT: BRANCH VI, 14 QUATRAIN 4 43

There shall be heard in heaven the clash of the weapons
Of the divine enemies in that year,
The sacred laws are unjustly debated.
The faithful will be put to death by thunderbolt and war.

Saran sentite in ciel l'armi combattere
Pur dei divini nemici in quell'anno,
Le leggi sante ingiustamente dibattere
I credenti per folgore e guerra, a morte metteranno.

Seront ouys au ciel les armes battre,
Celuy an mesme les divins ennemis,
Voudront loix sainctes iniustement debattre.
Par foudre et guerre bien croyans a mort mis.

Decryption

In the cinematographic strips there will be the harsh event of an atrocious month. If in the Seven all the churches join together to renew the age, from the Rose of the astral lights that come shall be seen the dissolution and annihilation of the demons.

In the Eternal City troubles will diminish if the machines from the sky lift the churches that will fall silent in the Seven out of divisiveness. If there is a true synthesis, it will coexist with a new and luminous man.

I see a malevolent servant of that harsh age annihilated. In the dreamlike city they climbed mountains of filth. You will never see the heavens there, if they forget to hear the sacred masses in their houses with the undesirable wine that so annoys them. Thus they renew an extensive plague among men. They annull the light, following the path of evocations. It is an aberrant way they take if they scale mountains of stolen relics.

If the extraterrestrials help us to clean out our dens, supported by the penetrating sound of rotors, now the traitorous earthly world will be extinguished. If they do not watch the bestial genital sense, our Mother can then come to all men. Thanks to the Councils of the city, fear of the extraterrestrials will perish, if the Tyrrhenians come to celebrate the Holy Mother. Too late to be redeemed from earthly errors, the drunkards will die.

Then everyone in Italy will be smiling, and no sad deeds will be heard of again. The kingdoms will then timidly return to serenity. They already had regency, but if the light is administered to us from the sacred base, it will be the time to embrace Christ.

PART VI

The Song

OF THE HEART

KEY TEXT: BRANCH XV,
11 PROPHECY 32 NOVEMBER

Lovely and shining, Venus will move into Flora.

The secret subverters will abandon the square.

Many widows are made, and the death of the Great one lamented,

But the mighty Power offers no threat to the kingdom.

Subentrerà lucente stella a Flora

Nascosta eversione abbandona la piazza,

Troppe vedove e del Grande morte si deplora,

Al regno ostilità il gran Grande non minaccia.

Venus la belle entrera dedans Flore.

Les Exilez secrets lairront la place.

Vefvues beaucoup, mort et Grand on dèplore

Oster du regne, le Grand Grand ne menace.

PLATE 66: ON HIGH WE SEE THE WHEEL OF NOSTRADAMUS, SYMBOL OF CHANGE. THE STAR, THE MOUNTAINS, AND THE SUN, ALONG WITH THE LION WEARING THE RED CARDINAL'S HAT (AS DID JOHN XXIII), SYMBOLIZE THE POPES OF THE SECOND HALF OF THE TWENTIETH CENTURY AND THE VATICAN COUNCIL'S RENEWAL OF THE CHURCH. THIS IS THE PRELUDE TO THE LIGHT OF THE GREAT SUN OF THE NEW MILLENNIUM AND HUMANITY'S REBIRTH.

KEY TEXT: BRANCH XV, 12 QUATRAIN 4 14

The sudden death of the first personage
Will change the kingdom, put another on the throne
Who swiftly and late climbs so high while so young
That both sea and earth will tremble at his journey.*

---

*See G. Conforto's book, *Giordano Bruno and Contemporary Science,* published by Noesis in 1955, for a detailed examination of the twin soul and the alchemical marriage in his chapter on "Utopia and Love."

La morte improvvisa del primo personaggio
Per cambio al regno un altro metterà:
Tosto e tardi venuto così in alto in bassa età
Che terra e mar staranno a paventarne il viaggio.

La mort subiette du premier personnage
Aura changé et mis un autre au regne:
Tost, tard venu à si haut et bas aage,
Que terre et mer faudra que on le craigne.

KEY TEXT: BRANCH XV, 8 QUATRAIN 8 36

Committed it will be against the anointed one,
From Lous le Saulines, Saint Aubin, and Bel'oeurre
Paving with marble from the towers taken
Not to resist Bletteram and his masterpiece.

Sarà commesso contro il sacro ducato
Di Saulo, Sant'Albino e bel lavoro,
Pavimento del marmo di torri lontane spogliato
Resister non potrà ai blateranti ogni capolavoro.

Sera commis conte oindre aduché
De Saulne et sainct Aulbin et Bel l'oeuvre
Paver de marbre de Tours loing espluche
Non Bleteran resister et chef d'oeuvre.

The year of the three popes, 1978, has been amply explored in the published quatrains of Branch XV *(The Popes of the Second Half of the Twentieth Century).*

Flos Florum, Paul VI Montini with the mountains on his coat of arms, died. Hidden subversion during the decline of Italy left behind it a swath of widows and sorrowful commemorations. However, the threats of a powerful nation ceased. John Paul I, Albino Luciani, seen as the light of a brilliant star or a rapid comet, was elected. His profound emotional response to the financial scandals in which the Vatican was implicated brought on his death. So yet another pope was elected, the Polish pontiff John Paul II, the traveling pope, the *De Labore Solis.* Like the Sun, he journeyed around the world.

The Lion of Saint Mark is on the shield of Pope Roncalli, who initiated a new historical course with the Second Vatican Council.

Soviet Russia did not support the violent actions of the Red Brigades, which culminated in the assassination of Aldo Moro.

Though his itineraries were disputed, John Paul II traveled constantly.

The Vatican suffered the plunder of its artistic masterpieces.

The Sun of the Prophecies Appears Today

From 1991 to 2011

QUATRAIN 1 48

When twenty years of the reign of the Moon have passed
For seven thousand years another will hold the throne,
When the Sun takes up the days he left behind,
Then my prophecy is mined and done.

This quatrain, in which Nostradamus announces the end of the validity of his own prophecies, when the solar race will pick back up the thread of history, is of the greatest significiance. According to a biblical interpretation, *Vingt ans* (twenty lunar years) corresponds to seven thousand years: "One day for one year, one day for one year have I given you" (from the Book of Daniel, 29.1 × 12 × 20 = 7,000.) Seven thousand years also could indicate the completion of an entire cycle of the history of the earth that is taking place today.

American psychic Solara* has confirmed that the ancient catastrophic prophecies of Nostradamus will no longer be valid when humanity becomes conscious of itself. According to Solara, we have precisely twenty years, from January 11, 1992 to December 13, 2011, to cross through the dimensional door that leads to liberation from physical bonds and to the birth of an era of joy. This perception is notably synchronous with the message of Quatrain 1 48: "For the Sun shall keep the law of the Great Messiah." Branch XXII, 2 Quatrain 5 53.

Great luminaries live in the sun, the seat of the solar race that incarnates periodically on earth and that now returns to pick up the history it had *left behind* and to which it had contributed. This time the solar reign will last for

---

*Solara, *The Opening of the Door* (Noesis, 1995).

seven thousand years, reversing the validity of the preceding catastrophic predictions and decreeing an end to them by its very existence.

The *computerized* decryptions cover a span of five hundred years. The beginning years of the next century will witness a reawakening of the messianic sun and the spiritual renewal of humanity.

Nostradamus also said that his predictions would endure until the year 3797, yet this is nothing other than a simulated date made up to satisfy the concrete thinking of his contemporaries. In truth, the prophetic texts in the form of the decipherment based on the "modulation of the phrases" have no temporal duration as we understand it, but a duration which is indefinite. According to numerology, 3797 = 8, a number that is the symbol for infinity. (3 + 7 = 10; 1 + 9 = 10; 1 + 7 = 8.)

In the letter to his son César, Nostradamus writes:

> In actuality we are governed by the Moon, through the omnipotence of Eternal God, and before She has completely concluded her cycle, She will reach the Sun and then Saturn. In fact, according to celestial signs, the reign of Saturn will return, for which reason by my calculations, the world is drawing close to an inevitable revolution.

In the quatrains, Saturn symbolizes the countries of the West. It appears as though the beginning of this revolution will come before the end of the millennium. In 1990 the signs of the coming of this revolution were already present and it is for this reason that Branch I of the twenty-first century coincides with Branch XXIV of the twentieth. When twenty years have passed (after 2011), Nostradamus's long-enduring prophecies will come to an end, leaving the world in the convulsions of rebirth. Afterward, a whole new humanity will emerge from the ashes of the old in the new millennium.

In his letter to King Henry II, Nostradamus made it clear that in the solar millenium of Christ prophesied in the Apocalypse "there shall be restored almost another reign of Saturn and a golden age: Satan captured, bound, and thrown into the abyss, into the profound pit" at which point his own prophecies of the destruction of the world would be "mined"—meaning no longer valid—and transformed by a self-aware humanity. This transformation appears very clearly in the deciphered texts where the disasters spoken of in the ancient verses are no longer in evidence, replaced instead by a sense of the effort of human renewal and what he calls *soluta oratione,* or the "resolved text"—the deciphered text that will now make the prophecies clear.

The sun directs the flow of the days that are left behind when they are not illumined by his passage. It is similar to saying that everything already exists in *memory* to be rediscovered and made manifest by the passage of the temporal wave, the present. Nonetheless, the days are always present, stamped into memory where there is no time, where past, present, and future coexist. The *memory of the future* has already been *left* where the seer or perhaps a special instrument can plumb it, bringing information out of atemporal memory and into physical reality by the interpretations of the quatrains, as well as by observation of the event.

Think of a radar screen, where little by little the luminous brush discovers preexisting outlines and objects. The Nostradamic-wave acts similarly, the difference being that its passage registers not the preexistent, but the wave itself, expanding into superdimensional memory. The seer has access to this global memory in which each part contains the information of the whole. The human psyche is such a structure, containing information from the past (memory) and the future, whose cause is in the present.

We human beings restrict our attention to the fleeting moment, defining as reality only the present; therefore the sun—or solar personality—obscures the moon, or global psychic sensitivity—which instead is connected to a more hidden interior sensation that includes in itself the past and the future. The moon signifies a listening to the interior voice, a perception able to receive information from all times. This is the hidden feminine wisdom: in the occult night the moon, represented in Plate 70 as the celestial Lady in the divine matrix of all things, possessess the completion of knowledge (see actual color figure, Plate 70). For this reason it is the moon that obscures the sun. Setting metaphor aside, it is possible to develop our own receptivity by quieting the noise of our diurnal activity and heeding the call of the inner voice.

KEY TEXT: PROPHECY/MILLENNIUM, 2 QUATRAIN 3 91

The tree that was dead and dry for so long
One night begins to turn green once again:
The king sickened by Time, the prince standing upright,
Will draw back the veil of the shrill enemy.

L'albero che per tanto è stato morto e secco,
Una notte comincia a rinverdire:
Del Tempo il re malato, in piedi il principe ecco
Dello stridulo nemico farà il velo scomparire.

L'arbre qu'estoit par si long temps mort seche,
Dans une nuict viendra a reverdir,
Cron Roi malade, prince pied estache,
Criant d'ennemis fera voile bondir.

In Salon-en-Provence, after the death of Nostradamus, a dead tree suddenly began to turn green and bear flowers. Here, however, Nostradamus is alluding to someone in the future who will suddenly provide great clarity so that the mysterious descriptions predicted in his verses will take on a logical and comprehensible form. "But the verses will do great damage," he added, because for the most part their interpreters will not be able to draw off the veil in which the quatrains were wrapped. There will come a day, however, in which they "will be made much more clear."

Decryption

Ugly linear time will come to put chains on the present. If the Lady will dispatch to the soul the clothing of love, you will have the pure path, even if obscenities dirty its name because of this heavy prison they carry.

If the intention is for a true utopia to come to all countries, this intent will illumine the dawn of reality. But if there is nothing but hatred and anger, this is the time when the Divine Lady will send her emissaries to redeem her name. The murderers who have all but destroyed the oxygen will die, those swindlers who seek an eternal utopia while bringing too many of their conflicts back to the East.

Wherever they are set down in new lands, women will be the ones to bring new joys and gladness to all men.

There will come a season of carnage and blood, since the pigs will seek to bind the just ones in chains. For this reason the king in the East will proclaim a hard rule to make you obey the old ideas. Tired of their burdens, some souls will happily accept in an instant the waves of the divine. Transcending predatory anger, they will create kindly islands. Many women will arrive there to work together on good new attitudes and to teach souls the greater reunions, accepting also that atheists by transcendence may reach the plane of the faithful. The sheep will escape the damage of the waste of the wolves.

In the regions of Lombardy they will teach that the souls from the south are worthy to come to them. If anger arises, think of making new agreements so that you may accept so many people.

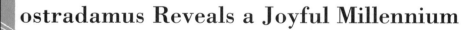

Nostradamus Reveals a Joyful Millennium

KEY TEXT: PROPHECY/MILLENNIUM, 3 QUATRAIN 9 87

> In the forest tilled of turf
> The temple will be placed by the hermit,
> The duke of the times for his found key
> From the mountain horizon will give the prelate example.*

---

*Translator's note: The above is a translation from Mr. Ramotti's Italian Quatrain, which differs from the original in some details. Following find my rendition of the original French, Quatrain 9 87:

> *In the Forest cleared of turf*
> *Will be placed the inherited temple,*
> *The duke of print by his invented ruse*
> *Will teach a lesson to the prelate of Mount Lehon*

Nella foresta dal tufo dissodata
Dall'eremita sarà posato il tempio,
Il duca dei tempi per sua chiave trovata
Del monte l'orizzonte al prelato darà esempio.

Par la forest du Touphon essarte,
Par heritage sera posé le temple,
Le duc d'estampes par sa ruse inventee,
Du mont Leh-ori. prelat donra exemple.

In a metropolis, a researcher discovers on his own a new method of organic reading of the quatrains.

The figure of the Hermit in the tarot deck symbolizes the researcher of all things occult. A scholar of the prophecies, then, inherits a spiritual temple in a forested zone "tilled of turf," which could refer to the houses built of blocks of turf that one sees everywhere in Lazio. "Heritage" and "ermitage" sound about the same and can be translated either way. The heir of the eternally wandering Hermit, that is, of occult research, will bring *the times of the popes into print* after finding this manuscript.

Lehi was an ancient prophet living in Jerusalem. The present sect of the Mormons in the United States is based on his inspiration. The key to the reading of the quatrains is derived with opportune modifications for adaptation to the Latin alphabet from the most ancient Cabala, which probably dates back to Melchisedek, who gave it to Abraham.

Decryption

That peace of which you now hear secret rumors is more likely to become history if the true sun will bear fruit. You will be given by grace a way to disseminate the joyful light. A gift of the people awaits you. The essence of the Millennium, whose philosophy will be revealed to you, is now predicting clearly dated events. In integrating the whole, a great thirst arises for a time of honor, for the truest and most luminous light. Wherever this light enters it shines for you, illuminating serene thoughts. This I foretell to you now, given that this echo is not distorted and the old destiny is turned around, placed under the Lady my patroness.

You will experience a worse fate and one that clashes with the Father if the errors of enacted evil are simply repeated. If some of your enterprises are to die, there are others weaving themselves that I have not been able to print. I believe a donor will come late to pay everyone and that they will receive millions of lire so that one November the Millennium will heal all, if I reveal that I have woven other schemes. As a gift you have now a ready author of the best criterion, if the years of evil do not come.

If I truly reveal the power of the mind, you have the gift of being the author of the work and of more fully intuiting the sky of Selene. When the twin is there it is the tenth year.

Nostradamus even speaks here of economic riches for those who reveal hidden truths through their intuitions.*

The year of the etheric twin is approaching. Plato spoke of twin souls, as did Giordano Bruno. A great many human beings will perceive their higher selves, or inner divine essences, merging with their own souls; thus they will be readied for the alchemical marriage. This marriage is the indispensible condition for meeting one's twin soul, according to the tradition of the Rosicrucians.† Self-awareness will transform the probable destinies of humankind, which will then become its own direct author, fully conscious of the fate it is creating.

KEY TEXT: BRANCH V/MILLENNIUM, 21 PROPHECY 43

Virgins and widows, your good time approaches
And will not be at all as it has been claimed.
For a long time a new approach has been needed.
Careless pleasures engaged in again bring on the worst.

Vergini e vedove lungo tempo a voi s'appressa
Che punto sarà chi vi pretendera
Lontano si porrà di far novello approccio
I rilassati costumi una volta rimessi, il peggio verrà.

---

*In *The Celestine Prophecy* it is also stated that gifts and economic well-being will come to those who act on their intuitions and do it for love.

†Translator's note: A literal translation from the French of the last line of Quatrain 4 14 reads: "It will be needful for earth and sea to fear him."

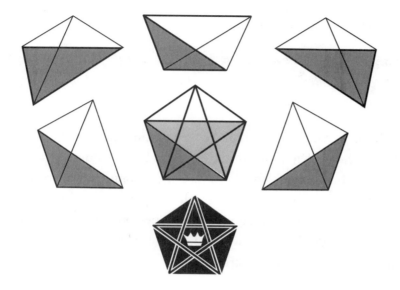

OUR MINDS HAVE THE POWER TO CALCULATE SUPERIOR DIMENSIONS. FIVE INTERLOCKED TETRAHEDRONS FORM A HYPERTETRAHEDRON IN THE FOURTH SPATIAL DIMENSION: THE PENTACLE, A FAMOUS ESOTERIC SYMBOL.

Vierges et vesves, vostre bon temps s'approche
Point ne sera ce que lon pretendra,
Loin s'en faudra que soit nouvelle approche.
Bien aisez pris, bien remis, pis tiendra.

Sexual epidemics and decadent customs will impede honest encounters between men and women. This quatrain, read cryptographically, seems like a newsflash from some sidereal journal set up to gather various bits of news from the future.

Decryption

At this time the pope becomes unpopular and a number of the blackest adversaries gather against him. This is because he distrusts the new philosophies, thinking that heresies could empty the churches. Regret for having pocketed money arises, but only in the penal objective; a very unpleasant chance will occur that will swiftly punish this man. The poor blacks will clothe themselves in Jesus once more, in peace and honesty, but when the African heresies rise again, He will be forgotten.

For fear of the independent philosophies, which are considered heretical by the Hierarchy, the pope concedes too much to African tribal rites in exchange for obedient devotion to the Church.

The criminal judges will weigh down your spirit if they always keep pardoning the wasteful squandering of religious sects; they will mend the endangered wall a little by means of the lira.

On April 30, 1995, the news reported a scornful reaction on the part of the Holy See to the declamations of the "Clean Hands" judges who accused the Church of paying scant attention to its ethical obligation of working toward a moral society. Accused of demagogy, the judges were invited to work "with legality and respect for the dignity of the person." But the corruption of politicians defrauds the poor whose lives by necessity are continually and unnaturally interrupted by maternities.

Conflicts will erupt when, tired of the ideology of the United States, you will turn to the Soviet Phoenix. A misleading vote of confidence is expected. They commit blasphemous and obscene offences, because they rehabilitate the thieves of the lira and we see the barbarous abortions of the poor once again.

In Israel, the sincere thoughts of upright whites full of rectitude will prevail, and in the name of charity they will give away their worldy goods in penitence. But when the harsh ire of the Zionists rises again, they will be greatly troubled by that inquietude. Then in October they can breathe.

They will give two TVs to the Israeli pacifists, hoping to fascinate them with seditious transmissions. As soon as the Zionists cease repenting, they will be seized in one disastrous coup by the PLO who will then in the winter steal various things belonging to the foreigners. The masters of the Western TV voices appear to be spies and the Iraqis and the Syrians will claim to cut off the transmissions, and it has been seen in the predictions that the fate of the PLO is to be struck down in a coup.

We shall be able to verify the truth of these predictions in the near future.

KEY TEXT: BRANCH XX, 10 QUATRAIN 2 51

In London the blood of the just will be spilled,
The six of twenty-three burned by thunderbolt.
The ancient Lady moves out of the high place.
Many of the same sects will be killed.

Sangue dei giusti versato sarà a Londra,
Per folgore i banchieri di ventitre bruciati
La Dama antica l'alto luogo sgombra,
Di stesse sette parecchi eliminati.

Le sang du iuste à Londres sera faute,
Bruslez par foudre de vingt trois les six,
La dame antique cherra de place haute,
De mesme sectes plusieurs serront occis.

The matter of finance is picked up again, but the encoded message deals here with the theme of sexual aberrations and with AIDS.

Decryption

The Moon comes to save worthy people, if She can undo an aberrant energy. If they know how to uplift a rude faith, the victorious wheel of the UFO will rise to the Holy See. Dare to put questions to their saints. They will respond from many centers. In the Lion, in the year of joy, wise individuals will point out the pictures of free rights, which you will enjoy if all sexual aberrations are cured, desiring to renew useless faiths.

All respond that what is needed is a useful, precise eulogy to heterosexuality to inspire them to the sacred joys, and say that they are setting up islands of laughter right now, if they would but turn away from the aberration of Russia and renew their faith in life, abandoning the wicked wolf and placing no trust in the dark doomsday cries. If they dare to expand sane and healthy joys, sex is also allowed in reality. That the mystic philosophies of the churches and also the ethical visions they have there may fall away. They have risk there of AIDS, in the present century. In some lady who, being where there was no light, lost her skin. Content to have been set down in the black terrestrial ravine, they would have to contract painful diseases from sex because of an excessive obsession. Who has heavy, hot desires will have to let them fall, for I see that more cures will be given to you.

Heresies lead your bodies neatly into that ravine through a foolish permissiveness, which is understandable considering the ways of the church are more tiring. The ETs could penetrate the ethical See to reach whoever now washes away the stain of sin. They would do well in Europe also to take on some of the roses of precepts.

In the recent encyclical *Evangelicum vitae*, the theme of abortion is treated with vigor. The papal precepts are "roses"—divine gifts—that should come accompanied by a loving comprehension of human fragility. Moral sense can be augmented by that consciousness being shown us by our brothers of other dimensions or worlds who even now manifest themselves by our sides.

PLATE 74: A WOMAN ABORTS, ASSISTED BY OTHER WOMEN.

KEY TEXT: BRANCH IV, MILLENNIUM, 14 QUATRAIN 7 35

The big pocket will come to weep and implore.
In that time they will be deceived who elect him.
The Guide will not want to live with them,
Since they will have stolen his language away.

La grande tasca verrà piangere, implorare.
D'averlo eletto, ingannati all'epoca saranno
La Guida con loro non vorrà dimorare
Defraudata sarà da quei del suo linguaggio.

La grande poche viendra plaindre plorer,
D'avoir esleu, trompez seront en l'aage
Guiere avec eux ne voudra demoureur,
Deceu sera par ceux de son langage.

Decryption

The octopus will invade the masses if they choose the path of learning the works, deciding to invest more in the West than in Eastern Europe. A law that climbs to the horizon comes to impede them. You will have an Oriental dollar that will exert a stronger control than earthly logic can counter. There will be extensive maneuvers on the part of men from the East, also because the country folk will be left without roots. And if they lose them, that grievous destruction will give rise to the people's hatred. Their homesickness will further spread the error of the earthly communist.

You will know a hostile time if they withold the springtime of the works of wisdom from the people, and there will come to our nations masters who will eat the rations of their own flocks. Sorrow returns if the hostile people come. If you happen to condemn the invasions, know that they too depend on that law which you cannot hear. The good light must come to expand it and heal the burning heat. To remain linked to the earth, worldly valuables must fall away here.

If they want a duke, the matter is grave. If criminal law comes to condone the slaughter, then the very waves of the ocean shall rise up. The light will cease to bless the earth: if you do not nourish love here the gifts of Jesus will vanish.

They will think they are smelling the odors of spices if they set themselves to sniffing the naked women in the demoniacal Russian lands, whence will come rumors of dark conspiracy.

If we stubbornly insist on staying on the material level, the "spring of the works of wisdom" will not unfold. Instead we will inevitably submit to a new dictatorship of which harbingers are already rising in the East.

KEY TEXT: BRANCH XX, 11 QUATRAIN 6 22

In the land of the great celestial temple
A disciple dies in the name of false peace.
The deed will be an example of schism,*
False liberty will be everywhere flaunted.

---

*Translator's note: The third line of Quatrain 6 22, rendered straight from the French, would read: "Then the boat will become schismatic."

Nella terra del gran celeste tempio
Adepto a Londra morto per pace simulata,
Il fatto allor darà di scisma esempio,
Ché finta libertà dovra essere ostentata.

Dedans la terre du grand temple Celique,
Nepveu à Londres par paix faincte meurtry,
La barque alors deviendra scismatique,
Liberté faincte sera au corn et cri.

This sidereal news item refers to the death of the banker, Calvi, who was found hanging in London in June, 1982, under the arches of the bridge of the Black Brothers. Calvi's wife is certain that her husband did not commit suicide. She believes that he was led on with false promises and killed. It is true that the Masonic Order, of which Calvi was a member, is hardly an example of real freedom, for the reason that it uses its secret as its cover.

However, after the work of the Anselmi commission, P2* split off from the official Masons, rendering its actions more transparent.

In Quatrain 2 51 combined with Plate 75 (which according to the keys of order are conjoined), we can see a clear connection to the contemporary financial activities of the IOR,† the Vatican bank, in relationship to the Calvi/Ambrosio Bank scandal. On July 28, 1982, the Vatican turned all legal and judicial communications over to Monsignor Marcinkus and two other members of the IOR, and spontaneously compensated the creditors of the Ambrosio Bank for over 250 million dollars.

Decryption

If the brothers renew the future clay to undo black and secret realities, so the delinquent pagans will give back the astral life. Even here you have the Father near you in the divine sea, though the Tiber holds the harmful waters of the enemies. The victorious heresies of the rebels will squander those charities that they continue to give them again and again. The papal age of gifts of money and acquired artwork, paid for by the priests, is coming to an end. This will frighten the enemy who will suffer from an enormous fear that by so impetuously lifting the veils they will receive the Holy Supper; and also that while throwing off the poison of arid money they will equally renounce future spending. There is the risk that the papal throne will fall.

In Rome there will be robberies and crises of the CEI,‡ as well as benefactors. If they harvest evil in their houses, they will betray the holy reasoning of the IOR (the Vatican bank). Those useful to them will be ordained, to the Latins they will give nothing.

Various harsh and disturbing denouncements will punish them for letting worldly interests and money ruin that bank. There is thought of accepting a foreign source of funds to help in recovering, which unleashes total conflicts in the city. The Roman Curia [Vatican Secretarial Administration] will consider resigning and will stop receiving their entitlements in lire, but if they stay here to burn candles we risk the Saracen beasts entering the CEI. The era will come to an end, but if they pay close attention the year the dead rise, the Sea will warn us of an insane fight.

---

*Propaganda Two, a masonic lodge accused of tormenting revolutionary movements in Italy.
†Instituto Opere di Religione (Institute for Works of Religion).
‡Conferenza Episcopale Italiana (Italian Episcopal Church).

KEY TEXT: BRANCH IV,
5 PROPHECY 104

Sprightly point, sweet fury in the heavens
You swell by three-fourths and die on the side.
The failure is witnessed, being but halfway to heaven:
By seven and three, and by one fifth to run.

Nessuna gioia, ma doccia furiosa al Sacro
Tre decomposti, all'accostarsi del quarto morire.
Viaggio fallire, non resta che la metà del sacro
Che per la settantatre e settantacinque trascorre.

Alegre point, douce fureur au Sacre
Enflez trois quatre et au costé mourir.
Voye defaillir, n'estre à demy au sacre:
Par sept et trois, et par quinte courir.

This quatrain corresponds to the plate on manuscript page 73 (+2). It foretells
the end of the pope's journey after the three popes of 1978 have passed on.

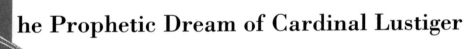

The Prophetic Dream of Cardinal Lustiger

KEY TEXT: BRANCH IV, MILLENNIUM,
4 QUATRAIN 6 86

The day after the great Prelate's dream
Is interpreted in reverse to its sense,
A monk from Gascogne will arrive suddenly
And make them elect the great Prelate of Sens.

Un giorno appresso al sogno del grande Prelato
Interpretato al rovescio il senso,
Dalla Guascogna a lui sopraverrà un monaco
Che farà eleggere il gran Prelato di Sens.

PLATE 76: A MONK HOLDS A CROOK IN THE SHAPE OF THE CROSS OF LORENA, THE SYMBOL OF THE "FREE FRANCE" OF DE GAULLE IN THE 1940S. THE MONK LEANS ON A STICK, SURROUNDED BY KINGS AND CARDINALS; A POPE SEEMS NOT TO WANT TO ACCEPT THE PONTIFF'S CROOK. AFTER A FALL, POPE JOHN PAUL II TOOK TO USING A CANE. (SEE COLOR PLATE 76.)

LUNEDÌ 6 MARZO 1995

Le grand Prelat un iour apres son songe
Interpreté au rebours de son sens,
De la Gascogne luy surviendra un monge
Qui fera eslire le grand Prelat de Sens.

Sens lies in the outskirts of Paris, not far from Fontainebleau.
From *Time* magazine, January 1995:*

And then there is another prominent convert: Jean-Marie Lustiger, 68, the Archbishop of Paris. Lustiger was born a Jew, the son of Polish émigrés

---

*Translator's note: This newsclip will inevitably differ in some words and constructions from the original published article, since it is the English translation of an Italian translation of an American magazine's report.

to France (his mother would die in Auschwitz). Abandoning his original name, Aaron, he adopted Catholicism as a teenager, a move that hurt his parents terribly. Lustiger is a trusted confidant of John Paul's; when he first visited the Pope, John Paul's secretary, Monsignor Stanislaw Dziwisz, grabbed the Frenchman's arm and told him, "Remember, you are the fruit of the prayers of the Pope. The Pope prayed long and hard over his choice."

Asked by *Time* about his chances of succeeding John Paul, Lustiger replies, "Me? Totally excluded. Out of the question." Lustiger fidgets silently with his breviary in its brown leather case, then suddenly announces, "I had a dream. I dreamed that the President of the United States was black, the President of the ex-U.S.S.R. was a Muslim—and the Pope was Chinese. And in my dream I asked God to let me die before that day would come. Because if ever we had a Chinese Pope"—he clenches his fist and makes a screw-turning gesture—"they know what administration is!"

Decryption

The solar pope could renew the good people if they considered firmly uniting their homes with the Holy See in the eternal present. If repressions smite them to cage the dissident pastors, good priests will leave the pope alone. They will stand in opposition when women are condemned to mate with the black goat, when women start turning away the earthly energies that are tearing them to pieces in the present. Denounced as whorish in their very essence, they will lack the basics in their homes by which to console their loved ones if they must suffer the weight of the papacy. Inexorable condemnation of women priests is the holy pronouncement. And I do not see the sweet Sun coming into the people of the future if the Holy See scorns every lunar interest; and those who have an anemic personal soul will err gravely. Parched with thirst, they will abandon themselves to impure dreams.

There will come from the north, from the oppression of laicism, a wolf of the omnipresent reign of money. Gratis, the Lord gave Europe back the powerful bridge of divine love. But now this Jewish Slav cardinal arrives to stir up a dispute by announcing to the faithful that women students would harm the organ-

ism [of the Church]. They are clinging to absurd hopes if the base, raucous crowd of the Right invites itself in. They will start quarrels even if a new generation comes to render the women well and whole, with no more need to lie. The cardinal is already manifesting harsh hypotheses of repression. Let us pray that the stellar sea will give love to women, not shouts of sirens and lesions, and by illuminating her, make her young once more.

The "sense" interpreted "in reverse" is also that of female sexuality, object of ancestral, Semitic fears. Frequently in the deciphered texts, the term "basic" is used to describe the true essence of womanhood. If lunar sexuality is to be the base of a sane existence, the importance of both sexes must be recognized, not debased in the banality of spreading materialism and consumerism.

No longer will women be prohibited access to the priesthood. If we wish to finally evolve we must convince ourselves that the body is not in eternal conflict with the spirit, with the soul, but in harmony with the loving whole.

Jesus lived among the ancient, patriarchal Hebrews and therefore could not gather female disciples. But when Peter reproved him for having spoken of heavenly things with Mary Magdelene, Jesus replied that he would like to have made her "as one of you." Let us hope that day will come soon. Once they are no longer forced to lie, one can foresee a great change in women themselves, for already their atavistic insecurity, the fruit of dependence, is disappearing.

They will be beloved as spiritual guides even more than men. This is already occurring in many places, but not yet in the Catholic Church, although the Church should perceive very clearly the advantages of such a change.

KEY TEXT: PROPHECY/MILLENNIUM, 25 QUATRAIN 5 49

Not from Spain, but from old France
He who will be elected for the trembling boat
Will give his trust to the Enemy,
Who during his reign will cause a cruel plague.

Non dalla Spagna, ma dalla vecchia Francia
Chi sarà eletto per la tremante barca
All'Aversario sarà data fidanza
A chi nel suo regno farà peste crudele.

Nul de l'Espaigne, mais de lantique France
Ne sera esleu pour le tremblant nacelle,
A l'ennemy sera faicte fiance,
Qui dans son regne sera peste cruelle.

Yet another old-style pope will arise, though he will stop short of the Spanish Inquisition. A malign fate will burn both books and the pontiff's cross of Lorene. Many will turn their backs on the pope. Women wish to enter the priesthood.

KEY TEXT: PROLOGUE, 13 QUATRAIN 10 91

In the year one thousand six hundred and nine a Roman cleric,
At the start of the year will elect
One gray and one black, from the Fellowship chosen,
Who have never known malice nor cunning.

Al Codice del Milleseicento il nono il Romano clero
All'inizio dell'anno fara elezione
Della Compagnia di un grigio e nero
Che mai vi fu d'un sì malins il nome.

Clergé Romain l'an mil six cens et neuf,
Au chef de l'an fera election:
D'un gris et noir de la Compagnie yssu.
Qui onc ne fut si maling.

The ninth pope, at the beginning of the new century, will emerge from the Society of Jesus, or will at least be affiliated with the Jesuit order.

Decryption

Of uncertainty born, concealed dissensions, brawling fights, and the shouts of students of the Furies return. Many were the sects to which I refused to ally myself.

Not born of the Latin people, this mission comes from their false arts of lifting up the brain. The light will not return, if the office will not be permitted to those who are in agreement with us, but the priesthood intends to be stingy about admissions. If they teach false philosophies, it will be to stir up dissension in their wicked servants. It is not by using insane concepts that the divine light will come to fill the chalice.

If the Church perceives and transcends its delusions, the madness of the senate and of the governments and ministries will also be cured, releasing them from their thankless roles. Or the Church may be cast out with troubled cries. That internal exile is even now foreshadowed by the economy, since in May they scheme to make omissions from the final financial balance.

The investigated sons appear to accuse the councillors of polluting their honest obligations. Until they are joined together, there will be deep divisions. A bone-chilling cold comes over me; I expect an era in which many exiled sons create trouble, confounding honest men. They will cut short the symptoms of improvement.

Many groups dedicated to esoteric research will not be equal to their task. They will prefer to take sterile counterpositions in a damaging sectarianism that will thrust them back into the shadows. There will be division even within the Church. The mad politics of money, placed above all other things, will cause the downfall of many Catholic prelates.

KEY TEXT: PROLOGUE, 14 QUATRAIN 10 54

Born in this world to a hidden handmaiden,
Twice raised on high by disastrous news,
Inside his enemy he shall be imprisoned,
And then conducted to Malins in Brussels.

In questo mondo da nascosta ancella nato
Il due volte innalzato per ferali novelle,
Entro il nemico sarà imprigionato,
Condotto poi da Malins a Brusselle.

Née en ce monde par concubine fertive
A deux hault mise par les tristes nouvelles,
Entre ennemis sera prinse captive,
Amenée à Maling et Bruxelles.

Decryption

Then there will come a colorless, illusory kind of destiny. In Europe they will assault the rites if they get the gloomy class of technocrats, which Italy can give them. I see that they block the signal of the old basics.

To make myself miserable I assist at the assault on the enemy column. A miserable fate will come to the Tiber, which a tenuous veto will oppose until the black sects assail them and put off the ancestral supper. Now I see the Holy See seduce many brothers. A humerous idea of how to finish them off comes to the compassionate enemy: for a change of environment, they will send a tailor to the great door that few intruders enter, to steal the art. These infiltrators have no integrity. They will try to sell off in auctions the paintings they so graciously relieve the refectories. You will see how well they can trim them down. But the seat of the ancient stole will change, if it begins once more to bring the ideal toward serenity.

If the Jubilees are prostituted, a misunderstood conflict over taxes in the churches will come to an end. If a yet greater tyrant comes along, I expect to see an insane separation, one, however, that will highlight happy lives. America arrives to ennoble the Renaissance Quirinal, as if it would shine more brightly if they spent money on it. It is arduous to make a list of the luxuries, the terrible irrecoverable wastes of wealthy America. A better Jubilee would instead bring about tolerance in the open sea of reality.

The exaltation of an arid technology blocks spiritual elevation, encouraging corruption and theft. A confirmation of this was printed soon enough in the Roman newspapers.

On April 28, 1995, robbers sneaked into the Vatican offices by forcing open the front doors. They stole seventeenth-century paintings, foreign currency, precious objects, and more. Ironically, Nostradamus had counseled a trimming down of luxuries of the priests, as well as a new tailor to reduce the pomposity of their vestments. The Church is not to consider the great Jubilee of the year 2000 as an occasion to make money.

On Good Friday, April 14, 1995, a Protestant woman pastor took the place of the pope, for the first time in history, during the celebration of the Via Crucis. The clerics read the Passion of Christ and it was transmitted on television around the world.

KEY TEXT: BRANCH VI, 16 PROPHECY 67

Occult inspiration will result in good:
Religion, peace, harmony and love.
The solemn wedding poem is not for everyone to sing.
The high will finish low and from on high be hung.

L'occulta ispirazione avrà buon risultato.
Religione, pace, amore e concordia.
Il carme nuziale non da tutti intonato.
Gli alti in basso finiti e dall'alto messi alla corda.

Desir occulte, pour le bon parviendra.
Religion, paix, amour et concorde.
L'epitalame du tout ne s'accordra.
Les haut qui bas et haut mis à la corde.

PLATE 78: A MAN AND WOMAN, BOTH IN VESTMENTS, HOLD UP A BOOK ABOVE WHICH HOVERS AN ANGEL ON A CLOUD. BEHIND THE MAN STANDS A SMALL NUN HOLDING THE PAPAL CROOK.

Decryption

From afar, where your thoughts come from, where the obstacles of egoism are less troubling to the honest heart, you will hear once more our sincere reminder. You will invite the kindly heavens down for your enjoyment. The more groups there are who give praise, the less your fear of the tomb will haunt you. Where love is, the limbo of death falls silent.

Where you do not wish to banish hatred from the Realm and still the quarrels, you will lead them to run amok in an insane brothel of fraud and irreparable damage, and I am more frightened still if they will have groups of initiates. As soon as a worse death threatens their bodies, the more you will see their panic arise. They will beget a mongrel quarrel and shed much blood in order to learn the lesson: the more they remember the warm master, the more they will be invited to play the flute.

The way of shouting and screaming acts principally to set these groups on an eternal, blazing path of death. Whenever they are troubled by an ugly crisis, it touches you intimately, because then you will run the risk of the lethal toxin. Improve their lives now, warning them that if they fall back into the abyss of a

fetid water, their lives will burn once more. It is a dark coffin you have up here for those who are fond of their own throats, thanks to the thought of the lives of the millionaires.

Now all of them must wake up, for the ugly crisis has begun here, since they themselves suffer death due to slavery to the millionaires.

KEY TEXT: BRANCH IV, 6 QUATRAIN 1 15

Mars threatens us through force of war.
Seventy times he will cause blood to spill.
Equal ruination will come to the clergy
And more to those who will learn nothing from them.

Marte per bellica forza ci minaccia
Settanta volte farà il sangue spandere
Eguali rovine saran per l'Ecclesiastico
E più a color che da lor nulla sapranno intendere.

Mars nous menasse par la force Bellique
Septante fois fera la sang espandre:
Auge et ruyne de l'Ecclesiastique
Et plus ceux que d'eux rien voudrant entendre.

This quatrain refers to the images after Plate 70 (+2): the events of the end of the millennium.

Decryption

They are thinking of breaking into the artworks of the museum, because when the king is elected, the troops will deceive him. A pope will vacillate if a strong tycoon snatches away his believers. He will make himself the sacrifice. The phase that makes the restless sons rave will pass. It will weigh heavy to spend money because of the mistakes of the master they put there. These restless sons will have a pope annulled who hopes to make money on an easy deal.

Having seen the ship weigh anchor, they leave the country and the lost government, and in the end their intense rage will beseige and strangle the miserable See in the leap year. If the pastor thinks he can share in oblique heresies, he is in error. Trying to block the celestial oracle of the Moon only spreads the affliction.

PLATE 79: THE CLERGY IS HACKED TO PIECES. THE ARMY INTERVENES. THE POPE LEAVES THE CITY AND GOES INTO EXILE. (SEE COLOR PLATE 79.)

Just yesterday they wiped out the peace of Pope Pacelli, since an anarchic autonomy rose on the instant, and the Holy See will regret it. If the silence of the seductive angels is allowed to well up once more, they will avenge themselves in the exhausted house of the heretical Furies. When fate decreed their descent, they delayed being reborn in order to become your heirs.

Seeking peace here, the bridge of the heavens will also descend, if you choose to understand more about the source of the problems in Europe over the years. You will see the events that come out of Russia.

Just so, in France, what was destined to be was born from the source of a bloody revolution. In people's homes peace will be in the horizon of the stars, and if we receive and incorporate the lunar antennae of the ETs, whosoever believes may design this destiny. When everyone can freely acquire a voluntary understanding of causes, the bridge of the Lady's ways will unfurl in descent.

Every constriction generates rebellion and anarchy, but connection with the Divine allows us to become masters of our own destiny, with a greater awareness of the causes of humanity's errors.

KEY TEXT: BRANCH IV, 12 QUATRAIN 10 76

The great Senate finds guilty of pomp
One who will then be expelled and defeated.
His adherents will be at the sound of the trumpet
Made public and by enemies driven out.

Il gran Senato riconosce la pompa
Ad un che poi sarà vinto e cacciato
I suoi aderenti saranno a suon di tromba
Ben pubblicati, dai nemici scacciati.

Le grand Senat discernera la pompe,
A l'un qu'apres sera vaincu chassez,
Ses adherans seront à son de trompe
Biens publiez, ennemis dechassez.

Decryption

There should come the exemplary weight of medicine, which Leninism taught to try to understand what a feat it is to leave the dark riches to Caesar. In the Realm, the Supper of the holy bread falls silent. They will have a bitter sermon if the Romans tire of giving, if the money they give disappears in the year 2,000, and the hymns of the Church will be heavy.

The causes of trouble arise from accumulation of wealth. The Roman Curia [Vatican Secretarial Administration] *will have to fire the clerics. In the Church they will even try to run the Senate. The sacred house must lose its money if the ship is to be derailed, because they have nothing to salvage from their useless needs but weight.*

The exhausting requirement for pomp beseiges that king. Yesterday's puerile desire to touch aristocratic Caesar must cease. Know that on the first day of the Holy Year, an American bank will collect the Romans' paintings, threatening to close down the seat of the Church. I know that I am sowing a sense of pain, but it is accompanied by friendly clouds. From the crisis will arise a divine discontent, so that if they repent, the Left will not take their decorations. The Right could heal the See, even if a dubious patron robs them completely of their riches. The solution will be seen and the rainbow born if the dominion of big business falls away. If they come spontaneously to work toward peace I feel that the Sun will rise.

But I think that if they steal the Madonna's adornments, they will land themselves in more trouble.

It is difficult to "render unto Caesar that which is Caesar's." Never was there a more ignored evangelical precept in the Church. Soon the Right and the Left will share among themselves the ecclesiastical wealth, but they must at least respect those objects of devotion dedicated to the Virgin Mary.

KEY TEXT: BRANCH IV, 16 QUATRAIN 1 04

A King shall be made in the universe
Who will not stay long in peace or life:
Then shall the Fisherman's boat be lost
And governed to its own great detriment.

Nell'universo sarà fatto un Monarca
Che in pace e in vita non starà lungamente
Allor si perderà del Pescator la barca
Sarà governata nel più gran detrimento.

Pars l'univers sera fait un Monarque
Qu'en paix et vie ne sera longuement:
Lors se perdra la Piscature barque
Sera regie en plus grand detriment.

Decryption

You shall see more anarchy when the loyal counselor perishes. In one moment of bad luck, the quiet of exile will befall that honest priest whom they censure. He will be surrounded by generals who deceive him in funereal livery. A frightening fanaticism has been reached by the time he comes to reign. You will have requiems and exile, and it will bode ill for the rites of the Church, but the phenomenon of these troubles is caused by the return of a dark, mindless atheist, who makes the people unreachable and inept.

More misadventures will befall the ship before the fearful storm is done. When social imbalance climbs to the fore there will be people shouting and crying before a better man comes along. In the space of a moment the attacking forces will take over the eternal paternal keep, and the Latins will encourage them to smash it. Even the pope will be revealed to have helped misfortune by gathering inspiration in unexpected ways. That saint will not be content to reside in the See. It is natural to neglect the kingdom if once again it makes the sons frightened and stirs up anger and gives me less of an opening. He will scream about razing things to the ground, mounting war, roasting the mortals alive if they will not leave their material reigns. He would even like to birth rigid spokesmen, praying that they turn to aberrant ways, disturbing women's ideas. He will invoke truce so that the tensions and anxieties which I see in the pictures of the times that I give you, if my prophecies come true, will come to trouble the women most of all. May the lunar event, by becoming real, bring them to redemption.

I do not care to comment on facts that will soon enough make themselves clear. An attentive rereading of the decryptions will bring on the light of clarity. I have friends, both men and women, who understand very well how to read the decryptions. In these times this inspiration naturally reaches all who want it.

All that remains at the end is a joyful prediction of peace.

KEY TEXT: BRANCH IV/MILLENNIUM, 8 QUATRAIN 3 67

A new sect of philosophers
Who scorn death, gold, honor, and riches
Will not be confined behind German mountains.
Supporters and reporters will follow in their wake.

Una nuova setta di filosofi
Disprezzanti morte, oro, onori e ricchezze,
Non confinanti coi monti Germani,
Ai lor seguaci andranno appoggi e stampe.

Une nouvelle secte de Philosophes,
Mesprisant mort, or, honneurs et richesses,
Des monts Germains ne seront limitrophes,
A les ensuyvre auront appuy et presses.

A new philosophy emerges—neither Lutheran nor Calvinist, but born of the New Age of awareness—which will bring to us Petrus Secundus, the new Peter of Christ.

Decryption

Swiftly, a new art expands, which the doctor described in the time of past, iniquitous tempests, to correspond to that which I draw for you in my old manuscript.

If it is permitted me to sort things out from the ledge of the faithful celestial sentries, I would that a healthy love would emerge from the Church and cast a sweet light wherever a useful plan needs expansion. The struggles of past events will vanish and, as they now have philosophies that help them, they will know brighter days in the order of the holes. A sign emerges that pessimism will not upset the balance of the world.

In reality you see the Church excessively adorn itself. I believe that Heaven would send out a simple, very ancient light if everyone would reject the poison of that dead weight today. I smile again at the thought of rich monsignors stripping themselves of their money if you see the philosopy that brings with it necessity's death.

If divine voices are lacking in Europe, the disasters will undermine the authority of the Church's ethics. You will hear lies and impious, misguided philosophies, even if honest people are there. May the reassuring lunar discovery permit them to reorganize the Country by extending themselves to assume it.

Economic depression hurts the Country if they venerate the ancient regents. Though lunar sex is permitted to all European women, they will hear on the television that they brought the lesion themselves if they have the presumption to brave the black shouts. An atypical plague is imported from abroad. The Country empties, if the poisonous enemy prostitutes enter, barely clothed; if the transsexuals give you opium, more transgressions will be birthed by their screams.

You must send the vipers away.

A sign of optimism appears in the divine voices, which many people hear, explaining the occult philosophy of the divine Essence.

Androgyny is not an expression of sexual degradation but of spiritual elevation.

The Time of the Androgynes

KEY TEXT: R.I./MILLENNIUM, 10 PRESAGIO 74

Saints saddened by the great brothels
Are suddenly gladdened by the Androgynes.
The majority cannot see the times;
Ever more of them will eat their meager meals.

Dei grandi bordelli i Santi malcontenti:
D'un tratto, per gli Androgini, più lieti diventati.
La maggioranza non sa vedere i tempi,
Quando a mangiar di magro, fra lor sono aumentati.

Les coulorez, les Sacres malcontens
Puis tout à coup par Androgyns alegres.
De la pluspart voir, non venu le temps,
Plusieurs d'ent'eux feront leurs soupes maigres.

Here the androgyne, the model of evolved humanity in the future millennium, is revealed to be a kingpin of the Nostradamic vision, a central pivot in his psychology. The androgyne is a member of a new angelic hierarchy that is developing even now. The human/angel embraces within itself the consciousness of both sexes and thus is freed from the stereotyped psychological gender roles to which it was "exiled" in incarnation. Although superior, the androgyne does not despise corporality nor, in particular, sexuality. Male or female, the androgyne engages in monogamous sex freely and with respect, without, however, being conditioned by it. In this way the androgyne is emotionally free to love without jealousy, because jealousy springs from the idea of exclusive ownership of another's body.

Love is cosmic and in the case of the couple, sexuality may or may not fulfill it. Love is enough unto itself and does not require return. Freed from the need to be loved in return, one may love everything and everyone without experiencing the suffering of abandonment and distance. There is no longer the necessity, tied to physicality, of leaving one beloved for another. There is instead the possibility of continually adding new *copain* (friends/companions) to the rose of relationship until a group is formed, a collective unity of love. Of course this will occur only in the case of evolved androgynes, while the majority of people will remain anchored to the traditional family model.

Already, one may find small communities here and there bonded by love, very different from today's nuclear families in which the worst tragedies are routine. This will continue until the advent of universal peace brought by the Millennium of Christ.

Decryption

When Selene, the Lady of the Moon, is met, she will give the wise gift of honest encounters between the two sexes. Then they will understand how to be alone. They will dare to say the only word that satisfies men immediately. From on high the light can bring a useful chance to the incarnate sisters. He painted a copain donné—given companion here—if I am able to understand some of the histories of the maidens—as if to speak of sex were a mistake.

The word of a less well-known lover fulfills the sisters whom I greet, saying that soon with the years men will leave behind the material world along with natural sex. When women comprehend the meaning of copain donné a well-

known wise man will come to help them. That natural sex may hide depravity is the error revealed to the sisters.

Do not support that story, so that the Bridge may reveal tangible advantages to the community, and if you keep good company there will be more to come. And let the point of our synthesis be understood: Wherever women have lost heart because of the crudity of men, the future will reveal no more suitors. If the scream of sex is still heard, they will know more trouble and pain.

Thus, a new use can be made of our kind of treasure by those who spend nine months in useless waiting. A rough and painful future for women at the passing of the Millennium. If you hope for a civilized society, the demands made on this sex will be severe. Even if they have heard the sound of many stories, nonetheless, it is a useless way to sow illusions among the mass of humanity. Make the last fears disappear and instead of a jealous possession you will attain a sex that is far more real.

Nostradamus seems to indicate a metamorphosis of sexuality and the process of reproduction in this decryption. Perhaps pregnancy will no longer be necessary. Regardless, there will be revelations about the nature of sexual relationships.

KEY TEXT: BRANCH IV/MILLENNIUM, 22 QUATRAIN 5 79

Now sacred pomp will have to lower its wings
Because the great legislator has come:
He will lift up the humble, suppress the rebels.
Some imitator will be born above the earth.

A sacra pompa si verrà ad abbassar l'ali
Per la venuta del gran legislatore
Innalzerà l'umile, vesserà i ribelli
Nascerà sopra la terra alcun emulatore.

Par sacree pomp viendra baisser les ailes,
Par la venue du grand legislateur:
Humble haussera, vexera les rebelles,
Naistra sur terre aucun aemulateur.

KEY TEXT: BRANCH IV/MILLENNIUM,
23 QUATRAIN 10 73

The present time along with the past
Will be judged by the great man of Jove:
Late the world will be left to him,
The cleric become a disloyal jurist.

Il tempo presente insieme col passato
Sarà giudicato dal grande Giovalista
Il mondo tardi a lui sarà lasciato
Il clero diventato uno sleal giurista.

Le temps present avecques le passé
Sera iugé par grand Iovialiste:
Le monde tard luy sera lassé,
Et desloyal par le clergé iuriste.

PLATE 81: NEW SEEDS SOWN, NEW VINES GROWN: THE NEW MILLENNIUM. (SEE COLOR PLATE 81.)

KEY TEXT: BRANCH VI/MILLENNIUM, 21 QUATRAIN 4 20

Longtime a place of prosperous peace will be lauded,
Throughout its deserted kingdom the fleur de lys:
Bodies dead by water will be brought to earth
To be entombed there in the hour of vain hope.

Per lungo tempo un luogo di prospera pace si loderà,
Per tutto il suo deserto regno il fiordaliso
Corpi morti il destino in terra porterà
Di speranza vana l'ora d'esser là sepolti.

Paix, uberté long temps lieu louera,
Par tout son regne desert la fleur de lys:
Corps morts d'eau, terre là l'on apportera,
Sperants vain heur d'estre là ensevelis.

Decryption

Then Jesus comes. In the land where the Redeemer will live as son and guest, all wars will end. There will be vigils for the angelic star. Having his roses as their reward, all people will be uplifted into the Sun, shattering their chains. The shouts of men will not frighten them wherever people of the groups can reveal the errors.

The lands will be given back to the upright if they will send previously chosen prelates to the long-awaited See of destiny. Abroad, where control will be better, the meek law of Jesus will return. Where they do not cross the Bridge of that Man who has already suffered pain for their sins, an artificial quarrel will arise from a mistaken sound.

Disaster will strike the See when that obtuse general, enemy of the churches, rises to power. Where today a Slav rules the Poles, penetrating further, they set up their duke. The sacred rites will come from Latin priests. Once the doors are opened, the exile of the pope will cure everything and quiet the suppressed resistance.

Now comes the era of the people who will change the old doctors. The land of the Knight's money will be renewed and the venal arts of religious rites will be balanced. The income of the priests will come to an end, the bequests of works of art will come to an end, because there will be a new kind of heredity. Seeing our priests continue to keep vigil, you will experience real recovery. Many perplexities will have to be resolved, having been lost in the legacies of artworks. Those who stay to listen to Heaven will come to honor our ancient ship.

PLATE 82: THE THREE
ESOTERIC VIRTUES. (SEE
COLOR PLATE 82.)

KEY TEXT: BRANCH VI/MILLENNIUM, 23 QUATRAIN 3 02

The divine Word will give to all substance,
Including sky and earth, occult gold at the mystic deed,
Body, soul, and spirit will be as omnipotent
At their feet as on the Heavenly throne.

Il Verbo divino darà alla sostanza
Compresi cielo e terra, oro occulto al fatto mistico
Corpo, anima, spirito aventi onnipotenza,
Tanto ai suoi piedi come al seggio Celico.

Le divin Verbe donra à la substance,
Comprins ciel, terre, or occulte au faict mystique
Corps, ame, esprit ayant toute puissance,
Tants soubs ses pieds comme au siege Celique.

The three women symbolize the three elements of which we are composed: the Body, the Soul, and the Spirit. Together these form the conscious, mystic communion of the fulfilled, projected human being.

Decryption

I see the light of the house of the oasis, but not in reality. I am announcing the complete revolution of the incommensurable sun of the esotericists, that at last the priest may love to bless the people's mouths. But when that flag reunited the architect of the houses of the theocrats, yesterday predictions came to me of killings, of a widowed house, with the icons of terrible struggles.

The "icons," a term that is also commonly used in the computer world to indicate symbolic profiles, are also the prophetic images of the manuscript of the Prophecies that concern the Vicars of Christ as perceived by Nostradamus in the fifteen hundreds.

Rome, named after a solar messenger, sends its sons afar to perform the sacred communion in their mouths, because the Church loves those that in reality have always practiced the precept. But there will be materialistic chances to add gold and ornaments to the altars. Thus does the serpent, the medusa, foment the destruction of the interior light.

The reduction of Holy Communion to the act of eating a material host gives rise to the danger of exchanging true divine connection for a banal formality, an automatic ritual rather than a means of being in communion with the divine.*

Nostradamus was still hearing the echo of the Renaissance and Baroque popes who strove to illustrate the magnificence of Heaven with stupendous works of art.

---

*For more on the Eucharist see G. Conforto, *Giordano Bruno and Contemporary Science*, Noesis, 1995.

The cities understood the sound of the oasis that came to console them. A visible nebula put the proud voices in a museum. When the epoch has a foundation for technical change, Rome will begin to look after the tracks of the stars in the sky.

This is a reference to the phenomenon of Nebula M51 in which the face of the celestial Lady appears, already noted by me in 1990. In 1992 the Hubble's orbital telescope discovered a cross in the center of Nebula M51, an incentive to "look to the heavens" for an understanding of those profound cosmic meanings of which all history on earth is but one manifestation. We are obviously not alone; there are beings from more highly evolved civilizations, aware of the times and ready for a contact with us for which we must prepare. Now.

If the loss, the separations from the skies of yesterday are eternally maintained in the lights themselves, the Prophecies may contribute to sow the seed of celestial vigils. If the school of oasis is set down in the Countries, if repatriation can peacefully break down the rituals of a pantheistic double, there is still a serious chance that the Son may come to visit humanity once again in your time.

If only everyone were moved by the announcement of imminent union with the Cloud, seat of the Lady mother of those ETs. Now it is to be hoped that you will learn to receive the message of the house, lexic, and understood as being very exact.

This decryption is truly an extraterrestrial contact of a lexic kind. The Cabalistic formula of cyclic rotation of the letters of the quatrains according to the sequence 1-5-5-5 can be applied to any text from a minimum of two to a maximum of six lines, with the intent of achieving this contact. However, the resulting decryption, facilitated by the use of a purposeful electronic vocabulary, must assume a mental materialization that is totally completed to obtain a wholly valid logical structure without incurring errors or confusions. It is necessary to rediscover *l'ars combinatoria* (art of combination), that dates back to the ancient Greeks, which was further developed in the Renaissance. I believe that this kind of decrypted reading may effectively constitute the foundation for a new, computerized esoteric school, an "access to the inexhaustible information systems of the Eternal Being."[*]

---

[*]Ken Carey, *The Starseed Transmissions* (San Francisco: Harper, 1991).

THE GREAT NEBULA M51* IN CANES VENATICI, NORMALLY SEEN IN ITS EQUATORIAL PLANE, IS A CLASSIC EXAMPLE OF SPIRAL NEBULAE. AN IMMENSE WHEELING SOLAR SYSTEM EXTENDING OUTWARD FOR 35,000 LIGHT-YEARS, IT IS LOCATED ABOUT 10 MILLION LIGHT-YEARS AWAY FROM THE EARTH.† M51 WAS FIRST PHOTOGRAPHED BY THE MOUNT PALOMAR OBSERVATORY IN THE 1950S. IN PHOTOCOPIES SUCH AS THIS ONE THE CELESTIAL PROFILES OF THE LADY (IN THE CENTER) AND THE DRAGON APPEAR VERY CLEARLY.** ANOTHER IMAGE APPEARS IN GALAXY M51: AT ITS CENTER, WHERE A BLACK HOLE IS PRESUMED TO EXIST, WE FIND OURSELVES LOOKING AT A SHAPE MUCH LIKE THE CRUCIFIXION. "AND HER SON WAS TAKEN AWAY TO SIT BESIDE GOD AND HIS THRONE."‡

Hubble Telescope's Incredible Discovery

There is a Cross at the Center of the First Black Hole

"It's as if God had put a great big cross there just so we could find it," said Holland Ford of Johns Hopkins University and the Space Telescope Science Institute of Baltimore, commenting on the incredible photograph sent back by the Hubble orbital telescope. Right at the center of spiral galaxy M51, just where astrophysicists have suspected for some time that they would find a black hole, there is the shape of a gigantic cross, apparent proof that the black hole sucks in gas and interstellar dust, reducing the area around itself.

*Translator's note: M51 is known as the Whirlpool Galaxy.

†G. Cecchini, *The Sky*.

**For more on this see Rev. 12:5.

‡See Rev. 12:5.

Now comes the page of hidden work, that seed born now on the eve of chaos. The announcement of this tomorrow could perturb the masses among those extraterrestrials born in T. Ceti if, once the Countries are occupied, they were to spy on us. That is to say, a return to the homeland could be rendered possible, now that they have children, with the Lady in the Cloud and with less naïveté in the faiths.

The function of the illustrations of these prophecies is to inspire us to leave behind the old rigid and dogmatic logic of the Church and to embrace a new and broader, cosmic vision of humanity. This is the perspective from which the papacy of *Petrus Secundus* must be understood, considering that *secundus* not only means "second" in Latin, but also "happy." It is a stimulus, therefore, to direct our attention toward our capacity for transformation in such a way as to create an opportunity for the Son, Christ, to return. The "pantheistic double" indicates the possibility that Christ will not be an individual this time, but the inner Christ—the superior human being, aware in the consciousness of Christ. The multitemporal vision of Nostradamus is a passionate one, dense with a new science that contemporary physicists will soon make clear. Albert Einstein was their precursor with his discovery of relativity of time, but he remained anchored to the idea of one time alone. Today, however, we are swiftly arriving at the hypothesis of temporal multiplicity.*

The Ills of the Body Without the Soul

KEY TEXT: PREFACE/MILLENNIUM, 40 QUATRAIN 2 13

Body without soul shall be sacrificed no more,
Its day of death set at hour of birth:
The spirit divine will make the joyful soul,
Seeing the Word in its eternity.

---

*See Ilya Prigogine, *The New Alliance,* Garzanti, 1978.

Il corpo senza l'anima piu non sarà in sacrificio
Il giorno della morte messo in natività:
Lo spirito divino farà l'anima felice,
Vedendo il Verbo nella sua eternità.

Le corps sans ame plus n'estre en sacrifice,
Iour de la mort mis en nativité
L'esprit divin fera l'ame felice,
Voyant le Verbe en son eternité.

The Law of Love will be everywhere triumphant. Our bodies will no longer be objects of sacrifice, because even in the material world we will be able to perceive lives beyond the confines of the earth, thus preparing ourselves intuitively to participate in life immortal.

Decryption

A month of satanic pains will scream through them if they get the idea of enmiring themselves in the sex of misguided heterosexuals. What is more, their women will have syphilis. The men wish to put off the wool of their monks' habits so that earthier men do not suppose them to be unnatural and impotent. They will think that the monks are eunuchs if they see them dressed as holy men. Extended too far, this ethic can be unreliable, but if the Father sent down his Son to die, it means that He wants to save humankind. An insecure lover will give you lesions if the art of the scream of sex is invoked in excitement. If you penetrate foreign women with the sexual arts, you must expect a threat to your lives.

The idea men have is that the sudden illness is God's fault, that he wants to reform the women and heal the men by putting them back in the celibate's habit. Men will heal themselves if they avoid letting the tyranny of dark desires for women into their hearts, because the women have painful lesions in their flesh. It is enough to find out the esoteric faiths of these jubilant sisters, because anger will thunder when the bad life is born.

There will be a discovery there that will draw out the poison. Then a better flesh will renew the laws of the civilized world. All the beasts will fall quiet there.

There will be widespread epidemics of sexually transmitted diseases, like herpes and AIDS. A remedy will be found, however, and the epidemic halted.

KEY TEXT: BRANCH VI/MILLENNIUM, 22 PROPHECY 73

Justice sent from the heavenly throne comes to France,

Divine Virtue brings peace to the whole Universe.

They will soon enough find a new way to spill blood

By the fire of aircraft, not by my verse.*

Giustizia messa da trono celeste che in Francia arrivare

Pacificato per virtù divina l'Universo

Ben presto trovan modo di sangue buttare

Per fuoco di velivoli, non certo pel mio verso.

Droit mis au throsne du ciel venu en France

Pacifié par Vertu l'Univers.

Plus sang espandre, bien tost tourner chance

Par les oyseaux, par feu, et non par vers.

The seer seems to be excusing himself here: The disasters we have borne and must continue to bear are not caused by his predictions, but rather are the hard price we must pay for our aggressions—for the rigidity of our conviction that we must either defend or attack, for our historical habit of resolving conflicts through war, and dropping bombs. Our catastrophes do not result from the prophecies, but from a humanity as yet unaware of itself.

In this decryption we find an exhortation to the clergy not to become involved with the glitter and tinsel of wealth, vanities that render faith arid. They should engage instead in "the eternal art of the modulation of phrases." Usury and other insanity will lay waste to Russia, imposing a renunciation of the divine, "molded by the empire of gold as in Peru." Deluded women will insult the "lunar art" of their sex with dark and heavy rituals. Other troubles will result from Asian cults: "The Bear will give them a bad day yet."

Then the glorious light of consciousness will be restored "by Orion, with synchronous reign." The celestial Lady will put a stop to the troubles. "From the heavenly spheres will be given you a new path to the eternal House." Our successors "will hear these chronicles once more" as they come true in the world.

---

*Translator's note: A literal rendition from the French of the last line would be: "By birds, by fire, and not by verse."

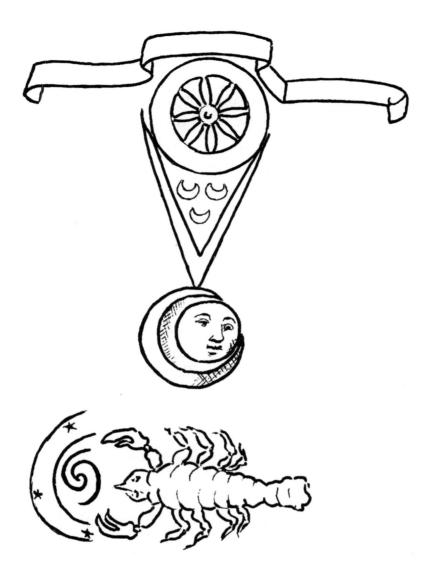

PLATE 70: THE MAN IN THE MOON IS WHAT THE ANCIENTS SAW IN THE MYTH OF ENDYMION, A LOVER OF ALL THINGS OCCULT. THE GREAT MOTHER APPEARS IN GALAXY M51 IN CANES VENATIX. UNDER THE SIGN OF CANCER, GREAT EVENTS OCCUR IN THE MILKY WAY, WHICH IS IN OUR GALAXY AND SOLAR SYSTEM. THEY LAST FOR THREE CYCLES OF THE MOON. THE GALACTIC SPIRAL IS CLEARLY SHOWN IN THE PICTURE, ALTHOUGH THE GALAXIES WOULD NOT BE DISCOVERED UNTIL THE TWENTIETH CENTURY. THE RIBBON OF STARS AT THE TOP COULD BE THE SYMBOL OF THE MILKY WAY OR OF THE "PHOTON BELT" MOVING TOWARD EARTH. (SEE COLOR PLATE 70.)

Astronomers have seen a photon belt in our own galaxy, which is surprisingly similar to the ribbon of stars in Plate 70. This photon belt is apparently about to enter our solar system and it is widely believed that its entrance will cause a great transformation to take place in humanity. According to channeled messages received by Virginia Essen, an American medium, our DNA could suddenly leap from two spirals to twelve.* Giuliano Conforto also speaks of

*Virginia Essen and Sheldon Nidle, *You Are Becoming a Galactic Human* (Santa Clara: S. E. E. Publishing Co., 1994).

the photon belt in his book *Giordano Bruno and Contemporary Science*, describing it as a gravitational prismatic lens.

KEY TEXT: BRANCH VI/MILLENNIUM, 8 QUATRAIN 6 24

When Mars and the sceptre conjoin under Cancer
A calamitous war will break out,
A new king is annointed a short while after
Who will bring peace on earth for a long time to come.

Quando Marte con lo scettro si troverà congiunto
Sotto il Cancro, sarà calamitosa guerra
Un poco dopo sarà nuovo Re unto
Che lungamente pacificherà la terra.

Mars et le sceptre se trouvera conionct
Dessoubs Cancer calamiteuse guerre,
Un peu apres sera nouveau Roy oingt,
Qui par longtemps pacifiera la terre.

A Mars–Jupiter conjunction in the sign of Cancer is predicted for 2002. The technique of *The Keys of Nostradamus* reveals a celestial image. Thirteen successive lines represent the recapitulation of the crucial numbers of the thirteen *Centuries* (twelve, and the *Prophecies*) in a rectangle of 13×100 dots, forming the synthesis of the Nostradamic algorithm I discovered. Do you remember the dot-drawing sent into space by the observatory in Arecibo? Its intent is to be understood, using a method extraordinarily similar to the one I attained completely by accident: a rectangle of 19×29 binary characters (black or white spaces) comprised of geometric figures that emerge from the disposition of the black and white holes.

And the reply to that message has effectively reached us from millions of light-years away, dropping 400 years in the passage, even though it is in the present that it has come to light.

The first figure on the left is clearly M51, a huge double stellar system whose points match the drawing's dots exactly. The left part of the diagram made me think of a stylized galaxy, but by observing its points I could see characteristics belonging to the outlines of real galaxies. For example, the rectangle on the lower right, present in both the drawing and the astronomic photograph, is very like the sign of Gemini. Although I overlaid the graphic design on several photos of different galaxies, only in the case of M51 do the points match exactly.

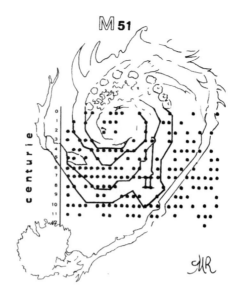

But that was not the only surprise. Once I had made a photocopy of the illustration, two images of disturbingly evocative power emerged as in a negative. Almost as it would appear on a medallion, in the center of the galaxy is the profile of a woman's face, her long tresses spilling over her shoulders, her head surrounded by a diadem of stars. Beneath her chin is a broad breach in the stars, like a monstrous mouth full of irregular teeth. At the top left are formations of stars like horns. "And a great sign was seen in the sky, a woman clothed in the sun, and the moon was under her feet and on her head was a crown of twelve stars . . . And another sign was seen in the sky, and this was a great dragon the color of fire with seven heads and ten horns and above his heads seven diadems; and his tail dragged a third of the stars of the sky and and hurled them down upon the Earth. And the dragon stood in front of the lady . . ."*

This is what John saw when he was borne up into the heavens. But who is it that sculpted this celestial image? It has existed for many thousands of years—since two galaxies approached each other in an extraordinary cosmic encounter—but only now, thanks to the telescopes of the twentieth century is it possible to see. The message that reaches us from this spatial abyss is yet more profound than the abyss itself. By evaluating the spatial perspective of the image, one can easily see that we are dealing with an extragalactic nebula, farther away than our own Milky Way. This means it can be observed without any appreciable distortion from every point in our galaxy—and not only by the people of Earth.

---

*Revelations, 12:1.

Apocalypse

KEY TEXT: BRANCH VI/MILLENNIUM, 25 PROPHECY 70

From "FAR DISTANT" time he will come to stir and
   arouse you.
Vain discovery against the infinite people.
Evil lurking unseen because of duty.
Found in the kitchen, dead and gone.

"LONTANO" nel tempo verrà suscitare per smovere.
Invano allo scoperto contro gente infinita.
Trascurato il male a causa del dovere.
Nella cucina trovato morto e finito.

De "LOIN" viendra susciter pour mouvoir.
Vain descouvert contre peuple infini.
De nul cogneu le mal pour le devoir.
En la cuisine trouvé mort et fini.

"FAR DISTANT" written in capital letters signifies the importance of temporal distance, the dimension of temporal passage that was permitted Nostradamus. Even the way his body would be found years later was precisely predicted. The keys of order place this quatrain at the end of the entire series.

Decryption

Gentleness will be born of this good new group of women. Living in the light, ever more faithful, they will try to fly and lift themselves up toward the ways of the sky. After the defeat of the serpents you will give up the pains of the tough, rotten apples till the gold of divine joy returns to the top, notwithstanding the standard bearer of a new duke who hopes to revive the fires of war and slaughter the faithful.

*   The Romans follow the subversives because of negligence. The Chiefs attempt some bloody missions to avert the night vigilantees of the Populists.*

The Vatican will not avert the danger of the subversive flame.

PLATE 72 (FORMERLY 70): THE ORIGINAL NUMBER OF THE PLATE COINCIDES WITH THAT OF PROPHECY 70, IN WHICH THE SEER EXPLAINS HIS TASK. THIS IS, THEREFORE, A SELF-PORTRAIT. THE MOEBIUS STRIP AT THE TOP SYMBOLIZES THE CYCLE OF ETERNAL RETURN FROM ANOTHER DIMENSION. AT RIGHT WE ARE SHOWN A WAY OUT. THE SYMBOLS OF THE CARTESIAN SPATIAL COORDINATES X, Y, AND Z ARE CLEARLY VISIBLE ON NOSTRADAMUS'S FOREHEAD. THE SMALL STAR OF INDIVIDUAL CONSCIOUSNESS WILL REACH THE SUN OF THE SPIRITUAL ABSOLUTE. THE WOMEN WHO LOVE THE MOON (THE DEER AT LEFT WAS SACRED TO DIANA, GODDESS OF THE OCCULT) WHO WERE IN THE PAST PERSECUTED AND CONDEMNED TO THE STAKE ARE NOW FORMING GROUPS OF LIGHT. (SEE COLOR PLATE 72.)

Harsh repressions will devastate them where they were taking steps to give out the light of faith and lost the Roman ecumenical hierarchy, which will perish because they take on ministers who are unbelievers. Now the surplices will more or less die out. In July I saw the heirs of the Romans down in the dust, avenging the dead women of those epochs in which they dispatched columns of women, sent them up in smoke to warn them to behave. The prohibitions reduce the flock almost to the point of sterility.

In reality Pope John Paul II condemned the stakes and funeral pyres of centuries past, but he was too late.

Then the light of the "time travelers" will come to open the mind. At the sign of Leo, more waves will come from which the divine models will emerge. The kindly ETs speak of virtuous ethics to the journalists.

A more comforting ethic will be given to us in a very agreeable way by extraterrestrial intelligences. In Plate 70 (formerly 68), the symbol of Cancer (the Crab) stands out, indicating that the time travelers will appear in July. Next to the spiral of galaxy M51 is a belt of stars through which such changes in time might be possible, in that they incorporate the presence of black holes or "cosmic lenses."

The sirens will wake up the arid houses and reveal the name of the ETs, whose faces they wish to know better. Wherever they have chosen subversion, you will hear the cries of the sad bazaars to which the stars will put an end.

At last even the political faiths of violence are destined to disappear.

A new race evolves as rapidly as the individuals who compose it develop their awareness of being multidimensional and eternal souls.

Apocalypse does not mean the end, but transformation.

The millennium, which is now drawing towards its close, is not only a date in the apparent physical world, but also in the real cosmic one, in absolute time, which beats not according to the constant rhythms of planetary rotations, but in accordance with the movements of evolution, expanding with the growth of consciousness. It may be sudden, instantaneous, eternal. Both incarnate and discarnate masters are always guiding us toward the path of Light that leads to the great and only Central Sun.

In this dimension of time-not-time, souls many consider themselves contemporaries if they have reached a comparable level of consciousness. In this kind of time there are many different possible ways of feeling and hearing dispersed throughout various moments of linear historical time, but it is important to know that all cosmic manifestations spring from a unified field in which the most diverse temporal rhythms coexist. It is in this unique field that the eternal present exists, expanding with the growth of human consciousness.

Nostradamus manifests this temporal multiplicity by putting his quatrains in apparent disorder, thus showing us how in reality the pictures of events we perceive are not tied to any linear temporal succession—although this too may be tracked through use of the keys to the undulatory order. The astral universe of feelings and emotions has its own times, as do the vital and etheric fields. All such emotions meet and entwine in the human being who, by evolving, will come into harmony with the unique wave, the fundamental harmony of the One.

Then we will begin to perceive the direct flow of universal Love from the Father, the Son, and the Holy Spirit, which will heal us of every ill, whether psychic, physical, or mental, and bring us to a place of perfection and joy.

The time-not-time of this evolution draws near. It is the time when terrestrial gravity will be overturned and change itself into heaven. It is the time of the Apocalypse, when all is transformed and revealed. The images in Nostradamus's manuscript, concealed for many centuries, have precisely this purpose: to help humanity comprehend the existence of those superior planes of consciousness which, in disregard of all linear boundaries, are forever traveling throughout time and space.

Index

solar verses, 79
soluta oratione, 116
Son, 5, 151, 152
Soul, 149, 161
Soviet Union, 114, 122. *See also* Russia
Spirit, 5, 98, 105, 107, 149
Stalin, 32, 98
star, 64, 67
stone of Turin, 71–72, 73, 74, 75, 80: cabalistic nature of, 84
Sun, 64, 79, 98, 139, 147, 160
sun, 116
Sun King, Louis XIV, 9
Sun of Nostradamus, 76
superior causality, 86
Syllabus, The, 20
synchronicity, 85

Tarbes, 61, 62
tarot, 119
Tau, 98
Taurus, 107
technology, 135
temporal distance, 158
temporal multiplicity, 6, 71, 85, 151
temporal sequencing of quatrains, 37–38, 64
temporal wave, 116
Theta, 99
Third Message of Fatima, 60, 61

Third Reich, 32, 92
three epochs, 5
three kings, 97–98, 99
three-pointed star, 97
three popes, year of (1978), 113
three stars, aligned, 13, 163
Tiber River, 72, 104, 105, 127, 134
time, 6, 85. *See also* temporal multiplicity
Time magazine, 129–130
Torah, 82, 83
towers, 43, 70
Tree of the Sefirot, 82, 83
Trinity, 5
Trojan hope, 49
Turin, 65, 80. *See also* stone of Turin
Turks, 51
Turkish Cypriots, 52
twin souls, 120

UFOs, 43, 102, 106, 108, 123
unicorn, 14, 37, 38, 40
United Nations, 50, 51, 53, 69
United States, 40, 67, 100, 102, 108, 122
Universal Council of the Church, 43
Urban VIII, Pope (Barberini), 2, 3, 4, 7, 11

Valois, 64

Vatican, 33, 54, 127, 135, 158
Vatican Council, 20
Vatican Secretariat Administration, 127, 139
Venus, 67
verbal waves, 90
Via Crucis, 135
Via Lessona, 84
Vicars of Christ, 3, 149
Victor Emanuel III, 33
Visto magazine, 106
Vittorio Emanuele II, 20

water (as destiny), 29
West, the, 51, 64, 68, 79, 99, 104, 105, 115, 122, 125
Western dagger, 64
Wheel of Destiny, 31, 38, 165
Wheel of Nostradamus, 76
wheel of time, 4
White Crow, 70
white magic, 65
wolf, 20, 78, 79
women, 107, 130, 131
women priests, 130, 131, 132
World Wars, 29, 31, 100, 101

Yeltsin, Boris, 70
Yugoslavia, 69

Zephirot, 84
Zionists, 122
Zirinowsky, 100